Men Read Newspapers,
Not Minds

Men Read Newspapers, Not Minds

...and other things
I wish I'd known
when I first married

Sandra P. Aldrich

Tyndale House Publishers, Inc.
WHEATON, ILLINOIS

Published in association with the literary agency of Alive Communications, Inc., 1465 Kelly Johnson Blvd., Suite 320, Colorado Springs, CO 80920

New Living, NLT, and the New Living Translation logo are trademarks of Tyndale House Publishers, Inc.

Scripture quotations are taken from the *Holy Bible,* New Living Translation, copyright © 1996. Used by permission of Tyndale House Publishers, Inc., Wheaton, Illinois 60189. All rights reserved.

Library of Congress Cataloging-in-Publication Data

Aldrich, Sandra Picklesimer.
    Men read newspapers, not minds—and other things I wish I'd known when I first married / Sandra Picklesimer Aldrich.
        p.   cm.
    ISBN 0-8423-8175-9 (alk. paper)
    1. Marriage—United States.   2. Marriage—Religious aspects.
I. Title
HQ734.A42   1996
306.81—dc20   96-9174

Printed in the United States of America

02 01 00 99 98 97 96
7   6   5   4   3   2   1

To two couples who have shown me marriage's great potential:

John and Elizabeth (Tibby) Sherrill

Bartlett and Margaret Hess

CONTENTS

ACKNOWLEDGMENTS

In 1993 I reluctantly accepted the invitation to speak to couples at the Christian Ministries Convention in Denver, even though I was convinced that married folks wouldn't listen to a *widow*. I labeled my session "Things I Wish I'd Known before I Married" and hoped that a dozen of my friends would show up. To my amazement, however, the room was packed, and I began to see that I wasn't the only one who had experienced more than a few surprises during the early years of marriage. This book was conceived at that gathering as numerous couples shared their stories with me, but undoubtedly it never would have been carried to term without my dear friend Greg Johnson of Alive Communications, Inc., bugging me about it. Then the birthing process was gently orchestrated by Kathy Olson, editor for Tyndale House Publishers, who made sure this "baby" was properly clothed. So, Greg and Kathy, thanks heaps! And may the Lord bless you both—and all those you love.

A WELCOME FROM SOMEONE
WHO'S BEEN THERE

Dear Friend,

Do you ever wish marriage licenses came with a warning label? I do, especially as my adult children, Jay and Holly, talk about their future—and as yet unmet—spouses. As I listen to and comment on their hopes, I'm remembering my own late-1960s courtship and marriage to their dad. And since I have a good memory, I'm more than a little concerned that they don't have a clue how difficult a good relationship is—just as their mother didn't. A good marriage is hard work.

Titus 2:4 calls for the older women to teach the younger women to love their husbands and children, so I'm willing to share some of the things several friends and I had to learn the hard way. I'm no "sweet, gray-haired little old lady." I'm a Clairol redhead who knows there's no tougher job than living in the same house with a person who can be absolutely, maddeningly difficult at times. But I also know there's no greater joy than working through the tough times and finding that you truly enjoy living with that person.

Perhaps you're skimming this book, convinced you don't have time to read it but looking for a jump start for your marriage. So here's a nugget: Recently Dr. Ron Cline, president of HCJB World Radio Missionary Fellowship, offered the ABCs of ministry partnership at a Colorado Springs leadership forum. Let's apply those to the ultimate ministry partnership—marriage:

A: Assumptions. Watch them. If you assume that your partner is going to act a certain way, you're in trouble. Things are never as they first appear—for good or bad.

B: Believe in your partner. Start with trust; don't wait to make the other person earn it.

C: Communicate.

So if you're engaged, newly married, or still trying to figure out this marriage thing after years together, come along. The following pages won't solve your problems, but at least you'll know you aren't alone in one of life's most maddening and most wonderful challenges—marriage.

Note: I've changed most of the names in the following pages—not only to protect the innocent, but also to keep the guilty from coming after me!

CHAPTER 1

Needed: A Marriage License Warning Label

A T the altar, the bride and groom smile at each other, convinced their marriage will be sweeter and better than any they've witnessed. They repeat the vows the minister offers or pledge their love from their own hearts, and they mean every word. They open gifts, looking forward to using them in a home filled with joy and peace. Then they're off to a honeymoon not only to consummate their new union but also to rest after the intense wedding preparations.

Bless their hearts; they don't know that the *real* work is about to begin. And all too soon one—or both—will have this fleeting thought: *But nobody told me it would be like this!* If they don't know that that sentiment crosses everyone's mind at one time or another, they may be tempted to bail out.

Remember the fairy tales of our childhood that usually ended with "and they lived happily ever after"? The stories featured the handsome prince and beautiful lady conquering problems that threatened to keep them apart—as though the main struggle was *before* the marriage and not the marriage itself. As children, we believed that once the couple had overcome all the obstacles—Snow White's poison-apple sleep and Cinderella's wicked stepsisters, for example—then the major battles were won, and the young lovers would live out the rest of their lives in sweet harmony, happily ever after.

Wrong. The real battles were just beginning. And one bright morning, even Snow White must have awakened early, stared over at the slack jaw of her snoring prince, and thought, *Who is this man?* And when Cinderella was pregnant with Prince Charming's baby, he undoubtedly stared at her swollen feet and wondered what had happened to those once perfect appendages that had sent him scouring the countryside for her. Nobody had warned them that swollen feet and snoring are normal parts of living "happily ever after."

Hilda certainly needed warning labels on her marriage license. As a child, she felt she didn't fit anyplace. Her classmates had mocked her old-fashioned name, and at home her parents didn't quite know what to do with this daughter who was their midlife surprise. But throughout her lonely teen years, Hilda held one thought close to her heart: Someday she'd meet someone who would truly love her.

That hope kept her company during high school and carried her into college. By then she had more sharply defined her future with her knight in shining armor, and at her job in the cafeteria dish room, she'd think about him: He would stroke her hair as he asked for the details of her day, and then they'd prepare dinner together before cuddling in front of the fireplace. In many of her mental scenarios, she'd stammer to him that she was talking about herself too much. But he would smile into her eyes, say he loved hearing the sound of her voice, and then kiss her eyelids and the sprinkling of freckles across her nose and say how much she meant to him. . . . And even though she occasionally scolded herself that there was no such thing as a knight in shining armor, she still dared to dream.

Then one morning, Jim, one of the new workers, smiled at her across a stack of trays. At their scheduled break, he introduced himself and asked her name. She gave it, but stammered that she'd never really liked it. He looked bewildered. "That's my grandma's name. She's fun. You probably are, too."

Smitten, Hilda began to look forward to going to work. As they continued to chat on breaks, they discovered they both were business majors and enjoyed tennis. By the time Jim asked her to attend a campus movie with him, Hilda had already priced china at the local department store.

They had a rapid courtship and were married a week after graduation. Quickly they settled into a new apartment and plunged into challenging jobs. But something was missing for Hilda: Her "knight" didn't call her in the middle of his busy day, and he didn't stroke her hair in front of the fireplace, and he certainly didn't ask for details of her day, including the office gossip. And their Saturday morning tennis matches had given way to errand running and budget balancing. In fact, come to think of it, she wondered if they had anything in common. This certainly wasn't the way marriage was supposed to be.

Meanwhile, Jim was bewildered that Hilda didn't laugh at his silly jokes anymore and was becoming more and more critical of everything he did. In fact, come to think of it, she had really changed from the sweet girl who had won him over with her shy smile.

Had marriage changed them both that much? Of course not. Hilda had married an image. And her "knight" didn't fit the picture of what husbands—especially hers—were supposed to do. And Jim had his own preconceived notions of what marriage should be like. Without meaning to, each mate had fallen short of the other's expectations.

A PERSONAL STORY

I understand those expectations. When I married Don Aldrich in the late 1960s, I thought he would make up for earlier disappointments in my life and that we would "do marriage" the right way. He didn't know that; he just thought he was marrying a Kentucky gal who knew how to cook. Obviously, we had more than a few adjustments to make.

I had met Don after an InterVarsity meeting at college. I heard his booming laugh and, smiling, turned toward the sound, determined to find the possessor of such joy. My life then was somber stuff to be plowed through instead of enjoyed. And suddenly there was someone who not only knew how to laugh but was determined to teach me how as well. It didn't take long after the wedding for me to discover that he met all of life's challenges with that same sense of humor, sometimes to my irritation.

I had also thought we would always do things together. After all, while we were dating, he had often rejected his friends' invitations in order to spend time with me, and I thought that exclusiveness would continue after we were married. Wrong.

I'm not the only wife who thought her man would want to be by her side constantly. I remember Kim's reaction when her husband of just a few weeks announced that he was going to play in his business's softball league. Kim had carried visions of long walks in the park each evening as they'd discuss their day and, hand in hand, dream about their future. The thought that her husband would rather be with a bunch of sweaty guys didn't fit her expectation of what loving couples did each evening. And she also didn't enjoy the idea that instead of handing him strawberries dipped in whipped cream, she'd be bandaging a different type of "strawberry"—on his skin and hard-won by diving toward home plate. Oh, she adjusted and accepted the fact that if she wanted to see him on summer evenings, she needed to attend the games, lugging along the lawn chair and watercooler. In time, she even started enjoying it and helped keep score. But that wasn't what she had planned when she went into marriage.

For Julie, another young wife who had read too many fairy tales, all of her unfulfilled expectations came to a head one evening as she and Dan celebrated their fourth wedding anniversary. For weeks, she had been looking forward to dinner at a fancy downtown restaurant, where diners enjoyed a view of the entire city, if one was fortunate enough to get a coveted window seat.

Julie had heard a wonderful course-by-course description of a friend's special evening there, but her own evening wasn't anything like the fantasy she'd set in her mind. First of all, her husband hadn't requested the coveted window table, so the maitre d' had seated them near the kitchen. Then the fresh gardenias hadn't been delivered to the restaurant that day. Julie's disappointment set the tone for the entire evening. Instead of concentrating on the fact that she was at the restaurant with someone she loved, she sprinkled her shattered fantasy onto her husband, letting him know that he couldn't do anything right if he couldn't even remember to ask for a window table—and why hadn't he made sure the restaurant had gardenias? Meanwhile, her husband felt unappreciated and more than a little disappointed in her as well.

SPECIFIC WARNING LABELS

So how do we keep unfulfilled expectations from spoiling a potentially wonderful relationship? By taking to heart these warnings:

Warning: Another human being can't meet all your needs
The only person who can meet all of our needs is the Lord, and he had to *die* first!

Carolyn and her husband recently celebrated their fortieth wedding anniversary. As I hugged her at the party that included numerous friends, relatives, and eleven grandchildren, she whispered, "I'm so grateful for our many years together."

If folks overheard her, they might have thought she was comparing her blessings to the scant sixteen anniversaries that Don and I had shared before Don's death. But I knew better: Early in their marriage, Carolyn used to take long walks—alone—and ask herself tough questions, such as *What are my choices? I don't want to raise these children alone. Is he really that bad a husband?* The problem was that he was just very busy building his business. He was trying to provide *for* his family, while Carolyn wanted him to provide *with* his family.

Mary, another friend, used to write long, unsent letters to her husband during his medical residency. Today, many years later, she's finally allowing him to read some of them. Together they can now chuckle over her young intensity that was trying to balance reality against her unfulfilled expectations.

Warning: The romantic level will not always be this intense
Several of my male friends like the old joke about the man who, on the wedding night, said to his bride, "I married you because I love you. If I stop loving you, I'll let you know. Let's not discuss this again."

While many men laugh at the account, most women are disgusted that their husbands just don't understand the importance of the spoken "I love you" that's accompanied by a gentle expression and a hug.

But we need to understand that the premarriage intensity cannot be maintained at the same level indefinitely. No one can sprint a marathon, and that's exactly what marriage is—a marathon.

Warning: Your spouse can love you and still not have a clue about what you need
Often as I talk with young wives, they lament, "But if he loved me, he'd know what I need." No. He can love you desperately and thoroughly and still not know what's bugging you. So it's up to you to tell him. Remember, if you don't ask, the answer is always no.

Clare was a new bride who was frustrated that her husband didn't understand how stressful it was to work in the marketing department of a major organization. Constant deadlines, stressful meetings, expanding quotas, and demands for new ideas left her exhausted at the end of each day.

Her husband, on the other hand, worked in a less stressful job and wanted to do "fun" things, including going to midweek movies. All Clare wanted to do most evenings was have a quiet dinner and collapse into bed.

When she mentioned her husband's lack of understanding to a coworker, the friend said, "Well, what does he say when you tell him how tired you are?"

Clare looked at her, aghast. "He should know how stressful my job is."

The coworker, a veteran wife, bit back a guffaw and encouraged Clare not only to tell her husband about her stressful days but also to work on finding activities that would relax and benefit both of them.

Warning: Your spouse will not always want to work on your relationship

If you'll forgive the generalization, women usually look for ways to improve even a good thing—namely their marriages. Men, on the other hand, usually operate with this thought, "If it ain't broke, don't fix it." The best way to counter this mentality, of course, is to compare marital checkups to the preventive maintenance that automotive owners should perform.

Warning: Marriage will not make you whole

One of my main themes at singles conferences is that when it comes to marriage, two halves do not necessarily make a whole. Often singles think if only they were married, they'd feel complete. So they put their lives on hold, waiting for future "completeness." For many, that means not only waiting to work on their weaknesses but also not buying the nice china, replacing a worn-out sofa, or even taking a fun trip, preferring to wait until they can share those experiences. Meanwhile, they're wasting precious time that could be used to perfect who they are already. The ideal marriage is a joining of strengths and a balance of weaknesses, not a demand that the other person make you feel complete.

Warning: You won't do everything together
Not if you want a healthy marriage. I used to think that marriage meant adhesion—because that's the way "loving" couples do it. Working together, planning together, setting goals together—all that *is* wonderful. But the relationship needs breathing room, too. If the husband doesn't want to see a "girl movie" (i.e., a romantic one), it's OK for the wife to attend with a friend and let him have a few hours alone. It's amazing how a little time to follow our separate interests can add energy to the marriage.

Mitzie loves quilts but knows that looking at colorful cloth squares isn't her husband's idea of a good time. So when the Pioneer Museum annual quilt-show arrives, she calls a friend for lunch and a tour. Good for her! I understand the pleasure that quilts bring, and I'm delighted that Mitzie doesn't give up her interest just because her husband can't be excited about it.

Warning: Marriage won't turn us into social performers
If we struggle with carrying on a normal conversation with people, getting married isn't the answer. Sure, our husband or wife might be especially gifted in this area and can help us out in group settings, but our weaknesses still need to be dealt with. For Margaret, that was one of the major insights after her husband took a new job. Previously, he was a teacher and had the summers off, so he took the kids to the local pool, allowing Margaret to concentrate on her home business and receive the neighborhood gossip from him. When his new responsibilities took him out of town, Margaret struggled with getting to know their neighbors for herself.

Warning: The only person any of us can change is ourself
If you're determined to change your mate, you're going to be

disappointed. That's such a simple concept that I'm amazed that not everyone has caught on to it yet.

The most common advice that married folks give to those who are dating is, "Pay attention to those things that bug you." It's a mistake to think you're going to do a makeover once the honeymoon starts. If something bothers you before you're married, it's going to bother you a thousand times more afterward.

Marriage is no place for constant criticism, nagging, or anger. Learn to live with the situation, or find some way to change *it*. But if your goal is to change the *person* causing the situation, you're in for a rough ride. For Lisa, who was frustrated with her husband's inability to see a mess, changing the situation meant hiring a woman from the church to help with weekly cleaning.

For Hilda and Jim, mentioned earlier, it took a Saturday morning blowup to open their eyes to what they had allowed to happen. It started simply enough: Jim wandered into the kitchen with the newspaper and reached for a cup, only to discover that Hilda hadn't made coffee that morning. She was savoring herbal tea as she read the latest women's magazine, coupon-clipping scissors close at hand.

Jim could have greeted his wife, made the coffee himself, and avoided an argument. Instead, he chose to voice his disappointment that she hadn't done what wives were supposed to do.

"Hey, how come you didn't make the coffee? You were down here first," he snapped.

"Well, good morning to you, too," Hilda replied sarcastically, and they were off and running into a major argument that included several *you never*s and a couple of *boy, have you changed*s followed by Hilda's tearful "This isn't the way it's supposed to be."

To Jim's credit, something clicked within him at that point, and instead of storming out to the corner café for coffee and solitude, he chose a wiser route.

"Look, let's start over," he said and backed out of the kitchen.

9

Then, standing in the doorway, he dramatically cleared his throat before saying, "Good morning, dear wife. My, but aren't you the picture of loveliness today as you clip coupons, sparing me from that mundane activity."

Even though Hilda knew he was kidding her, she smiled. He stared, then said softly, "I've missed your smile."

They weren't cuddled at the fireplace, and he wasn't stroking her hair, but as Hilda looked at her husband, she decided it was time to learn how to deal with this real man. And that realization provided a new start—and one that wasn't built on unfulfilled expectations.

SIMPLE REMINDERS

1. Unfulfilled expectations pose one of marriage's greatest challenges.
2. All too soon one—or both—will have this fleeting thought: *But nobody told me it would be like this*.
3. Yes, even swollen feet and snoring are normal parts of living "happily ever after."
4. Another human being can't meet all your needs. The only person who can meet all of our needs is the Lord, and he had to *die* first!
5. The romantic level will not always be this intense.
6. Your spouse can love you desperately and thoroughly and still not know what's bugging you. So it's up to you to tell.
7. Your spouse will not always want to work on your relationship.
8. Marriage will not make you whole.
9. You won't always do everything together.
10. The only person any of us can change is ourself.
11. Marriage is no place for constant criticism, nagging, or

anger. Learn to live with the situation, or find some way to change it.

DISCUSSION QUESTIONS

1. What expectations did you bring to your marriage?
2. Which of those expectations caused the greatest problems?
3. How did you work through the situation?
4. What have you learned from this experience?
5. What advice do you have for couples just starting out?

CHAPTER 2

Hey, This Is Hard Work!

S UPPOSEDLY I was concentrating on my potato-leek soup at our local café, but actually I was eavesdropping as the two women at an adjoining table discussed their marriages. The older one was complaining about having heard a speaker define a good marriage as "having the right partner and being the right partner." She went on: "But that way if a couple gets divorced, they can always shrug it off by saying, 'Well, I just didn't have the right partner.' That's why commitment has to be the basis of any marriage. Some days that's all that keeps any of us together."

I was tempted to sit at their table! I know about that commitment stuff because even as much as Don and I loved one another, we occasionally had days when we would have traded the other gladly for a gumball machine. But we were committed to the Lord and to each other, so we hung in there—and allowed ourselves and our relationship to grow. We learned the hard way that marriage is *not* a fifty-fifty proposition, but a seventy-seventy deal—and that's on the *good* days.

Dick and Rose Keilhacker know about that, too. It was the spring of 1966, and they were still struggling over the stillbirth of their third child, Johnny, just a month before. Rose's health had suffered an intense setback, but Dick had been attentive and strong for her. Now she wanted him to rejoin life, so when two fellows from their Sunday school class invited him for a round of Saturday golf, Rose insisted he go, saying that a morning in the sunshine would be good for him.

Within an hour, Dick's friends were helping him back to the house; his mouth was bloody, and several of his teeth were broken. A golfer on another green had blasted the ball right into the young father's face. This was the final straw for Dick. They'd lost the baby, his wife's health had been seriously threatened, his job at the steel mill was phasing out and forcing him into night classes, and they already had a stack of bills left from the funeral and no insurance for this latest trauma.

Already juggling all those crises, Dick began a series of painful visits to the dentist. Then repeated infections developed. And each new setback brought fresh despair.

One evening, Dick was slumped forlornly in the living-room chair. Rose watched him for several minutes, then pulled the ottoman close to his side. She took his hand and said, "We're going to make it through this, Dick. We still have two beautiful children and each other. When we started out, we had nothing but an old '54 Chevy with a few wedding gifts on the backseat. If we have to, we can always go back to that point and start over. But with the Lord's help, we *will* make it."

He looked at her for a long moment, then nodded and even managed a bit of a smile. "You're right," he said. "If it comes to that, we can start over."

That scene was a pivotal point in their marriage. Rose chose to encourage her husband in his lowest moment, rather than wring her hands and bemoan their fate. She grabbed an image she knew he would relate to—their old Chevy—and offered hope out of that.

Today, when folks meet Dick and Rose, they're impressed by the couple's warmth, their solid Christian maturity, and their deep love for the Lord and each other. They've come a long way from that scene: Dick has a doctorate and is now superintendent of a Los Angeles suburban school district, and Rose is the first woman president of the Los Angeles Mission Foundation. But neither has forgotten those difficult times and the importance of encouraging each other.

Recently, as they talked about those early challenges, Dick thanked Rose for standing with him: "You didn't say anything when things were bad; you just trusted me," he said. "The other men in the classroom reported that their wives complained about their long hours away from home, saying, 'Why didn't you go to school before we got married? Why didn't you get this out of the way?' But I never heard that from you. Your silent commitment was a real encouragement to me."

Rose was delighted by his revelation. "Some women might think I was giving him the 'silent treatment,' but that wasn't it at all. I'm a talker, and if I'm angry, I'll spew my thoughts all over. If I'm quiet, I'm at peace. I knew how hard Dick was trying, so why make the situation more difficult?"

Rose was far wiser than she gives herself credit for, though. She might not have understood the full ramifications of what she was doing, but through her silence she was acknowledging her love, her commitment, and her affirmation. Dick knew he could count on her in a crisis as well as in the good times. And that knowledge paved the way for the growth that followed.

THE AFFIRMED WIFE

Rose's affirmation reminds me of the classic story "Johnny Lingo's Eight-Cow Wife."[1] A South Pacific traveler heard an incredible account of a young islander named Johnny who had paid the highest possible bride price, eight cows, for a homely young woman. But when the traveler finally met her, the wife proved to be incredibly beautiful—not ugly at all. When asked to explain, Johnny answered, "Do you ever think what it must mean to a woman to know that her husband has settled on the lowest price for which she can be bought? . . . Many things can change a woman. Things that happen inside, things that happen outside. But the thing that matters most is what she thinks about herself. . . . Now she knows she is worth more than any other woman in the islands."

While I abhor the idea of women being purchased, I do enjoy this illustration. Because her husband loved and honored her, she blossomed under his love.

That's a remarkable reminder for all of us. Wives *and* husbands become the persons they are told they are. What if we poured love into our spouse? What if we stopped expecting perfection and allowed the freedom to fail? What if we bit back the quick retorts and put-downs that spring to our lips when we're angry? What if we acknowledged the good things our spouse has done instead of pointing out all our disappointments? What if we were determined to help our spouse be the person *God* intended instead of demanding what *we* want? What if we sent our spouse into each new day surrounded by our love?

GROWING OLD TOGETHER

Reminding one another of their love was something my Kentucky grandparents, Papa and Mama Farley, were good at. They had been married for sixty-one years when Papa was hospitalized during his last illness. Mama insisted on sitting for long hours by his bed, saying they'd never been separated and they weren't about to start now.

At one point they reminisced about their 1909 meeting at her cousin's house, where he had been a boarder and she had been the beautiful guest. When her two-week visit was over, they married.

As they talked there in the hospital room, eighty-two-year-old Papa took Mama's hand and said, "I don't want anybody to ever take you from me."

As Mama softly told the account after Papa's death, tears welled up in my eyes to think that their love was still so deep after six decades. And I was amazed, too, that Papa hadn't looked at her gray hair and wrinkled face; he saw the beautiful girl with the hazel eyes and Cherokee cheekbones that he'd married. Mama continued to hold that scene in her heart until she joined him in death nine years later.

It's every couple's dream to grow old together, as my grandparents were privileged to do. But there are some practical steps you need to work on now to make that a blessing rather than something you'd rather do without.

Recognize that men and women have different emotional needs
Women usually want to talk through a problem, while men, in general, need time to think and be alone. Too often we women try to get our men to talk before they're ready. We'll even follow them down the hallway, urging them for an immediate decision as they retreat from us. What if we tried leaving them alone for a while? And men, try to be sensitive to your wife's needs as well.

Barbara likes working through her decisions aloud. She'll argue first one side and then the other with anyone who is willing to listen. Hearing the various options helps her choose the one that will best suit her needs.

Her husband, Cody, though, prefers mulling over the various aspects of the decision and coming to his conclusion alone. If he is pressed for an answer, he will say, "Every wrong decision I've ever made, I've made in a hurry." Barbara quickly learned that the more she tries to hurry him—whether it's on what color to paint the kitchen or which elementary school their son should attend—the longer it takes. Now she presents the situation, offers a reasonable time by which she'd like an answer, and then gets on with her life. The home atmosphere is much less tense now.

Avoid nagging
A veteran husband once told me that nothing can wear him out faster than a nagging woman. I thought of his comments again

recently when I was a speaker at a writers' conference. The other speaker was a kind, gentle man, who was chatting with several of the staff when his wife showed up.

She stepped into the conversation with a quick "You didn't get a paper." Immediately he excused himself and hurried across the lobby to the paper machine. I watched with great interest, wondering why she, a physically healthy woman, hadn't felt capable of getting her own paper. Apparently she had it in her head that such a chore was *his* job, not hers.

Within a few minutes, he was back and handed her the daily news. She gave him an it's-about-time glance and turned to go back to their room. She didn't even thank him! She left him looking very much like a little boy who wanted to please someone who continued to ignore him. Would it have killed her to smile and thank him? As a widow, I watched, wondering what opportunities I had missed to show Don my appreciation. Undoubtedly many.

And while women are stereotypically the naggers, it's an easy habit for men to fall into as well. Let's all try to express more thanks and fewer complaints.

Find out what's important to your mate

I once took a woman's magazine quiz that asked what room I thought my mate wanted kept clean at all times. At the time, Don and I had two toddlers who were always scattering their toys around, so I thought he would say the living room. But when I looked up from the quiz to ask him, he immediately answered, "The bathroom."

I hadn't known that! He'd never said a thing about my hot curlers on the counter or the row of cosmetics lined in front of the mirror.

"What?" I said. "Why didn't you tell me that before?"

He grinned and said, "You never asked!"

So I started concentrating on the bathroom. Come to think of it, he *was* rather good at stepping over the living-room toys and never saying a word.

Don't flirt with anyone but your spouse

Boy, is this a big one. It amazes me that couples think they can flirt "harmlessly" and their mates won't be hurt by the special attention given to another. I'm convinced that more marriages are damaged by a mate's insensitivity in this area than by anything else.

Anne and Bernie had weathered eleven months of rocky adjustments as newlyweds when they attended a New Year's Eve party with several friends. After a pleasant evening of table games and snacks, the couples watched the big red ball drop on the Times Square television broadcast. As the thousands in New York cheered in the new year, Bernie put his arms around Anne and kissed her passionately. To Anne, the kiss represented sweet hope that the new year would be better than the old, filled with deeper love and greater commitment. With Bernie's arms still around her, Anne leaned against his chest, savoring the special encouragement that surged through her.

The moment was short-lived, though, as another guest, Kim, turned away from kissing her own fella and sauntered over to Bernie. "Happy New Year, big guy," she said as she kissed Bernie solidly on the lips. Then, to Anne's astonished disappointment, Bernie wrapped his arms around Kim and kissed her back. Suddenly, the embrace that had seemed so full of love and promise for Anne meant very little. The party was over for her in that moment—and so was the hope that the new year would offer a fresh beginning.

Jerry Jenkins, in his book *Hedges,* warns that even "innocent" flirtations have no place within the marriage: "Look around. Let your guard down, don't remind yourself that you made a vow before God and men, don't set up barriers for your eyes, your mind, your hands, your emotions, and see how quickly you become a statistic."[2]

Keep the respect alive

Respect is central to marriage, so don't say things to your spouse that you'd never say to a friend. Gail had the habit of griping at Andy every time they drove together. Instead of a casual "Would you mind if I turned the radio down a bit," she'd snap, "Must you have that so loud? Every time I get into this car, you have to have the radio blasting!"

Another friend, Roger, thought that his sense of humor was wonderful—even if no one else did. And he carried his jokes just as far as he could. One afternoon, he was at the apartment pool when his wife stopped down to let him know that she was going to run a couple of errands and would be back within an hour, in plenty of time to leave for the Sunday school party. She pointed out the fact that she was all dressed, so they could leave whenever he'd like.

Roger, with the sudden mischievousness of a nine-year-old, splashed her repeatedly, styled hair and all. And then he was upset that she was upset. A good sense of humor is wonderful, but childish pranks denote meanness—something that has no place in a marital relationship.

Talk—don't assume

Guys, you need to know this: Your wife loves talking with you. Many couples set aside fifteen minutes after dinner each evening to catch up on their day. Don and I talked after we put Jay and Holly to bed each night. We quickly learned the importance of three little words: three to say more often—"I love you"—and three more to eliminate—"But I thought . . . ," as in *but I thought* you'd be pleased. *But I thought* that's what you wanted. *But I thought* you'd already taken care of that.

That learning came the time we were driving to Florida to visit

Don's father and attend the Orange Bowl. Don had wangled the coveted tickets through great effort and put them in a safe place— the kitchen mug rack. As we left for Florida, he thought I'd gotten the tickets, since trip details were my specialty. Sure, I do details— but I don't do football. So forty-five minutes down the road, when Don asked me to check our seat assignments, I told him I didn't have the tickets.

"But I thought you got them!" he said. "I stuck them on the mug rack so you wouldn't miss them."

"Hey, I was doing everything else; you should have remembered the tickets," I retorted. "You're the football fan."

Then, thankfully, one of us (probably Don) was calm enough to suggest that we solve the problem rather than argue about whose fault it was. We discussed having Bill, a neighbor, use his key to get the tickets and overnight them to us at the Florida hotel. But what if they managed to get lost? Finally we decided that the best thing to do was turn around, drive back home, and get them ourselves. Of course that decision threw us off our schedule, but at least we had an immediate solution to our problem. We also learned from it: The next time game tickets arrived, Don immediately put them into his wallet.

Learn to communicate

After one couple's fiftieth wedding anniversary party, they were in the kitchen for their bedtime snack. Just as they had done every night for five decades, the wife made tea while the husband prepared the milk toast. But as he set the bowl of toast and warm milk in front of his wife, she suddenly burst into tears.

When she could finally talk, she said, "I can't believe that tonight of all nights, you would serve me the bread ends just as you've always done. After fifty years, I would think you'd show me more honor than that."

The gray-haired husband was bewildered as he softly replied, "But the ends are the *best* part."

What a difference it would have made in their marriage if they had communicated. How sad to think that for half a century, she never realized he was making a regular sacrifice for her.

Or how about this example? One of my friends tells about his buddy who was a professional football player for a number of years. His bride didn't like football, but she loved this gentle giant of a linebacker, so she settled into married life knowing he would be on the road much of the time. To meet their bills as well as to keep herself busy while he was gone, she worked two jobs.

After the season was over, she decided she had to have a talk with her beloved. So over his favorite dessert one evening she gently said, "Honey, I know you love playing football, but we need to think about your getting a job and helping with our bills."

With the spoon still in his hand, he stared at her as he realized that she didn't know he got paid to play and had been investing his salary for their future. And for the first time, he understood that she was working two jobs because she thought she *had* to!

He strode to his desk, pulled out his end-of-the-year check stub and handed it to her. "I do get paid," he said. "And I've been investing the money for us. I thought you knew that."

Delighted, she took the receipt from his outstretched hands, then turned back to him with a smile. "Why, honey, that's good that you were paid $25,000 last year to play football."

He leaned close to her. "Count the zeros, babe. Count the zeros."

As she turned back to the check stub, she saw that he had actually received $250,000! She quit both of her jobs the next day.

What a difference a little communication would have made early in their marriage—and their relationship. In fact, communication is so important that we'll come back to it in a bit and devote all of chapter 5 to this challenge.

STARTING TODAY

Perhaps you're thinking, *Yeah, all that stuff is good, but you don't know what I'm living with.* True, I don't know everything that's going on in your marriage, but I do know about the normal husband-wife tension. So let me ask an important question: Do you *want* a good relationship? Do you want a bad one mended? Are you willing to make the effort?

In John 5 when Jesus went to the pool of Bethesda, he approached *one* man to heal him, walking past numerous folks with desperate needs. Can you imagine being in a scene like that? (For me, it'd be like the children's game Duck, Duck, Goose. I'd run from person to person, thumping them on the head and calling, "Be healed! Be healed! Be healed!")

When Jesus approached the man, he asked a very important question: "Would you like to get well?"

You remember that the man didn't answer but offered excuses instead: "I can't. . . . I have no one to help me into the pool." It's as though he were saying, in effect, "Hey, it's not my fault; it's someone else's."

So, I'll ask you: Would you like your marriage to be healed? Or are you still offering excuses? And don't think your life would be simpler if you were single. I've been a single mother for many years, and I can assure you that there is no harder job in the world. So put your energy into working on this relationship—and making it as good as it can be. Sure it's hard work. But believe me, it's worth it.

SIMPLE REMINDERS

1. Some days, commitment is the only thing that keeps any of us together.

2. Marriage is *not* a fifty-fifty proposition but a seventy-seventy deal—and that's on the *good* days.

3. Rather than wring your hands and bemoan your fate, grab an image—such as your starting point with an old Chevy—and offer your spouse hope out of that.

4. Knowing that you can count on each other in a crisis as well as in the good times paves the way for growth.

5. Wives and husbands become the persons they are told they are.

6. Men and women have different emotional needs.

7. Most men would agree that nothing wears them out faster than a nagging woman. So be kind to one another.

8. Find out what's important to your mate.

9. Don't flirt with anyone but your spouse.

10. Keep the respect alive. Some days that's even more important than love.

11. Talk together. Don't assume anything. Communication is vital for all those who care about their relationship.

DISCUSSION QUESTIONS

1. What pivotal scene defines your commitment?
2. How have you encouraged each other in tough times?
3. When did you learn that marriage is not a fifty-fifty deal?
4. Do you both handle stress the same way? Give examples.
5. What have you learned about marital stress?
6. How have you learned to communicate?

CHAPTER 3

Children Don't Arrive by
Immaculate Conception

RECENTLY I spoke at a Saturday retreat in the Midwest. During the break, a lovely young woman approached. Her shoulder-length blonde hair set off dark brown eyes, and I found myself envying her flawless complexion. She took my offered hand, then whispered, "I really appreciate what you said just now about the importance of the sexual side of marriage, but I've gained so much weight after our three boys that I don't like my husband to see me."

The confession surprised me. "But you're beautiful," I gushed. She stared at me, wanting to believe my words. "I mean it," I assured her. "You are a lovely young woman. Sure, your body isn't a size eight, but it's produced three healthy little boys."

Wait. Slow down. I told myself. *Maybe her husband has a problem with her weight.* So I asked, "Is your husband upset?"

She shook her head. "No, he's wonderful about it. He acts as though I'm still the size I was when we married. The problem's mine. You ought to see him; he's gorgeous! And here I am!" She gestured toward her hips.

"Honey, stop putting yourself down," I insisted. "You *are* beautiful, so don't let those few extra pounds put a barrier between you and your husband. If you reject him, he's not going to blame your insecurity about your weight; he's going to blame himself."

Her eyes widened. "He's already asked what he's done wrong."

"And what did you tell him?"

"I said it wasn't him, that it was me."

I lowered my voice to match hers and gave her some woman-to-woman advice about what a husband wants, some of which I'll share in this chapter. As she blushed, I gave her arm a little squeeze. "Tonight, you just forget about the size of your thighs and love your husband the way he wants you to—and the way you want to. Make that man glad he baby-sat today so you could come to this retreat."

I gave her a hug then and added, "You're going to have one happy man tonight."

She smiled as she turned away, and there was a definite lilt to her step. Of course, I was curious about what would happen that night!

But later, I began to wonder if I had overstepped the Titus 2:4 bounds. I know Paul told the older women of the church to teach the younger women how to love their husbands, but I'm not sure he meant *that*. So I called one of my trusted young friends—a husband in his late thirties—and told him what I'd said. "Do you think I was out of line?" I asked him.

He enthusiastically supported my advice to this young wife and urged me to repeat it as often as I had the chance. So there you have it, ladies. I hope your husband is close by so you can put down this book and give him an inviting hug.

I want to stress that this chapter isn't going to solve all of the bedroom problems in the world. But if I can encourage a few spouses to respond enthusiastically to each other, then my sitting here typing with a red face will be worth it.

GOOD SEX

A few of my friends are more than a little horrified that I'm including this section in the book. Somehow they think that at my age or in my status as a widow I shouldn't be writing about this subject. Tell ya what, honey, I remember how my children were conceived, and I even remember what nightgown I was wearing (or *not* wearing) those nights. And as far as my age—well, the skin around my eyes may be wrinkled, but there's nothing wrong with my hormones.

Just whose idea was sex, anyway? God's. Our enemy, Satan, has distorted what was a great idea and turned it into lust. Proverbs 5:18-19 says, "Let your wife be a fountain of blessing for you. Rejoice in the wife of your youth. She is a loving doe, a graceful deer. Let her breasts satisfy you always. May you always be captivated by her love." Also, look at the Genesis account of Adam and Eve in the Garden of Eden, or at the Song of Solomon, if you need encouragement that God has blessed the physical union of married folks.

Jay and Holly used to be embarrassed that *their* mother would admit the importance of a good sexual relationship as she'd speak at couples' retreats, but they've finally given up trying to turn me into a "proper" woman. Besides, if they say anything, I just remind them they did *not* arrive by immaculate conception.

After their dad died, I put that good area of my life into a box and emotionally stored it away, planning never to see it again. Then about eighteen months after the funeral, we were attending the Gun and Musket Show at Greenfield Village in Dearborn, Michigan, where we enjoyed historical enactments by folks dressed to match the time period of their firearms. As I ambled across the village green toward the Civil War recruitment tent, a ruggedly handsome Old West cavalry officer strode toward us. From his black hat to his polished black boots, he personified masculinity. I was so taken by the sight, I breathed, "Oh, my!" without thinking. Apparently, he could read lips—or eyes—because he smiled and veered toward me.

Immediately I scurried away. As I did so, a new thought settled into my being: My husband was dead, but I wasn't.

That realization startled me, so in the days ahead, I clung to

Isaiah 54:5 with even greater tenacity: "For your Creator will be your husband. The Lord Almighty is his name!" And again I chose to shut down that part of my life. And as a single person, that's the only way I can deal with this issue—by not dealing with it. So I pour myself into Bible study, keep my eyes on the Lord, work hard, go to bed exhausted, and sublimate that sexual energy into other efforts—and continue to stay away from sensuous reading material, suggestive music, and the "adults only" section of the video shop.

But I'm assuming that those of you reading this book are married, so hear me: The physical relationship is very important to the marriage. Make sure you keep it uncluttered—and make time for it. In today's busy schedules, if something has to go, make sure it isn't your sexual relationship.

I love the story of the busy executive who left his wife a list of errands he wanted her to complete:

1. Pick up shirts from the cleaners.
2. Price cellular phones.
3. Buy five gallons of paint for the basement.
4. Call kid down the street about yard cleanup.
5. Call Fred about using his truck for yard cleanup.
6. Be wearing a negligee when I get home tonight.
7. If negligee is black, ignore first five items on this list.

A FEW REMINDERS

OK, let's get specific. Since I'm older, young husbands often talk to me, trying to understand their wives. Here are some of the realities I've run into:

Men want their wives to desire them sexually
In other words, he wants her to initiate sex more often. Now notice, the operative in that statement is "more often." Not every time,

because that puts too much pressure on him to perform. That doesn't mean that a wife has to rip off her husband's clothes—although he might like that occasionally. She may have to start slowly if this is a new venture for her—even giving him a gentle shoulder hug as he's reading the paper and adding a quiet, "I'm looking forward to going to bed with you." Ah, come on! Don't be afraid to have a little fun with sex. It doesn't always have to be serious and romantic.

Great sex for a woman starts long before bedtime
It doesn't start when she's brushing her teeth and thinking about crawling into bed. Usually by that point, she's just thinking about going to sleep. Her husband, however, can be intent upon reading the paper, paying bills, or watching a TV special and never give his wife a glance—and then suddenly be raring to go as soon as he steps into the bedroom. Women typically need more warm-up time. Even a brief hug in the kitchen as her husband helps clean up the table will help her feel gentle toward her mate.

One gal said, "My husband wants me to be a race car, ready to go from zero to ninety in ten seconds flat. But I'm an old Dodge that needs to warm up a while." A little kindness goes a long way toward starting her engine and keeping it running at an energetic purr.

Most women know this little secret: How she's treated out of bed determines how responsive she will be *in* bed. More than one man has been honestly bewildered that at bedtime his wife was still miffed over his criticism of the new dish she'd tried at dinner. To the husband, it's a that-was-then-this-is-now situation, while the wife wants that previous event settled before she can go to the next point.

Everything in the woman's life is wonderfully connected. That's the way we are made. We can pacify a toddler on our hip while we sort through the day's mail and suggest science project ideas to our third grader. Men, I've been told, compartmentalize everything. By virtue of the way God designed them, they often truly don't see the connection between what happened at dinner and what is *not* about to happen in bed.

But don't give up, women. Men *can* learn to understand the way we work. They can even learn how important it is to occasionally bring flowers home for no reason at all. "I saw these and thought of you" will do wonders for a lackluster evening. And so will his taking the children for a Saturday afternoon—after helping with the chores—just so "Mommy can have some time to herself." One man said if he had known taking the children for a couple of hours would do so much to restore his wife's sexual energy, he would have started taking them out long ago.

I do want to emphasize, though, that a mature wife is going to give her man some slack here and not nurse a grudge or pout or, worse yet, withhold lovemaking just because he didn't do everything right that day. It's important for both spouses to be forgiving toward their mate rather than childishly finding ways to make him or her pay for oversights, misunderstandings, and downright humanness. Keeping score of every little wrong is a good way to flame tension and dissatisfaction. And marriage already has enough challenges without adding that fuel to it. Occasionally, run your day's activities—and attitudes—through the measure of 1 Corinthians 13, the famous "love chapter." It's amazing how petty most of our grievances seem when compared to that standard.

Turn off the TV and turn on your mate

I am amazed at the number of hours wasted in front of the TV. What if spouses left the sets off each evening and invested that time in each other?

Pam says the best thing that happened to her family—and her relationship with her husband—was having the TV go on the blink the month they couldn't afford to repair it. They were forced to read, talk, and concentrate on each other.

Love is spelled T-I-M-E

Too many couples go from one frantic activity to another each evening. Somehow we can always fit what's "important" into our schedules—but some of us need to reevaluate the importance of a good physical relationship with our mate. In fact, it had better be rather high on our list of priorities. One busy wife sobbed to her friend after her husband left her for another woman, "Why *her?* She's overweight and not even pretty. Why did he start an affair with her?"

If she had asked him, her husband would have quietly said, "Because she has time for me."

Ouch. And in that same vein, more than one professional husband has asked his wife why she took up with a manual laborer and has received this answer: "Because he makes me feel important to him."

So don't take each other for granted. That part of your relationship is too important to let slip away. Schedule intimate time together. Yes, write it on your calendar if that's the only way to make it happen regularly. We make time for parent-teacher conferences, business trips, or picking up tickets for that special basketball game. Many folks spend more time pursuing hobbies than they do working to improve their marital relationship.

Don't compare your wife to another woman

Like the young mother at the beginning of the chapter, wives worry about how attractive they are to their husbands—especially if they've gained weight or if the stomach stretch marks after childbirth are especially bad. For Martha, those marks embarrassed her so much that she stopped undressing in front of her husband, Joe. When Joe asked her what was wrong, her reply surprised him: "I don't want you to see how ugly I am with all these marks."

Then Joe was able to assure her that he wasn't bothered by the marks. In fact, they were reminders that her body had produced two beautiful children.

Wow. Good choice of words, Joe, to build a bridge between the two of you. Not at all like Tim, who wanted to let his wife know that he liked looking at her body, so he bought a couple of "girlie" magazines and left them out where she would see them. Dumb move. Tim's wife interpreted his action as dissatisfaction with her body. And believe me, it's impossible for a normal woman to compete with those airbrushed, image-enhanced perfect women.

I remember Mario, a teacher who was working a summer job in our area. At lunch one of the men came into the lunchroom and asked, "Hey, did you guys see Miss July? She's something else!"

A couple of the guys nodded and grinned, so the original luster turned to Mario. "Did you see her?"

Mario dismissed the man. "I don't look at those magazines."

"Mario! You're Italian! How can you not look?"

He shook his head. "Those women have never had babies. How must a wife feel if she knows her husband is looking at another woman's naked body? I love my Rosa. I never want to hurt her like that."

The men looked at him as though he were from another planet instead of from another country. But every woman in that room sighed with new respect for Mario.

Know that children will greatly change the relationship

Why don't couples have a better sexual relationship? Many times the answer is plain old exhaustion. Don and I were married more than six years before Jay was born. Then sixteen-and-a-half months later, Holly arrived. (I add that "half" because I desperately needed those last two weeks of sleep before she arrived.) It took her forever to be able to sleep through the night, so for a long time I would put Jay and Holly to bed and then literally *run* to my bed.

I wanted to get to sleep *fast* because I knew she'd wake me up in about an hour. Those were exhausting times! Gone were the perfumed sheets and dimmed lights that set a romantic mood. Suddenly everything was out of kilter—and it looked as though it would never get right again. If young couples aren't prepared for those times of being needed by the kids constantly (and especially, it seems, in the middle of the night!) then those challenges can take a heavy toll on marriage.

But let me encourage you: These hectic days—and sleepless nights—are *not* going to last forever, even though they occasionally may seem as though they will. So talk together and decide what you can do to make this time more enjoyable. Often it's the little decisions that make a big difference.

For Norm and Ellen, it meant letting the housework slide and slowing the evening activities so they weren't exhausted at bedtime. Manny and Olive occasionally hired a neighbor girl to oversee supper for the children while they grabbed a quick sandwich and a walk around the block. Don and I would occasionally hire my sister Thea, an energetic teen, to stay over Friday night and allow us to sleep in on rare Saturday mornings. That proved to be the most successful arrangement for us. We had tried going to a hotel one weekend, but the unfamiliar bed wasn't comfortable, and our entire conversation centered on Jay and Holly anyway. Glenn and Dorothy similarly figured they'd never rest well at a motel, so they just traded baby-sitting one weekend a month with friends so they could sleep in and enjoy leisurely cuddling. But one thing got all of us through those times: We believed the relatives when they said, "This too shall pass." And it did.

Know what turns your spouse off
Many women hate it when their husbands wear socks to bed for an impromptu romp. Husbands, ask your wife what you could do to make her feel more romantic—it might be something that simple!

33

By the same token, several husbands have confessed that they can't stand their wife's flannel nightgowns. If that's how your husband feels, how about wearing the romantic one to bed and then changing into the flannel? Mitzie said once they'd made love, he never noticed what she was wearing because he was already snoring. One lingerie line finally got smart and designed a gown that's flannel on the inside and satiny on the outside. That way everybody's pleased.

Try some variety
How do you tell your husband or wife that you want to do something different? By suggesting it. You may have to take the initiative, wife, by directing his hands or affirming his action with a whispered, "Oh, that's nice." And husbands, you need to know that what feels good one time may not feel so good another time. For example, your wife's breasts may get tender the week before her period, so be especially gentle then, please. Both partners just have to keep in tune with what the other person's body is saying at that moment. But think of it this way: Not knowing exactly what is going to happen helps keep it interesting!

WHAT ABOUT THE "OTHER" STUFF?
What if your husband or wife is pressuring you to do something sexually that's making you feel uneasy? If it violates your personal ethical code, don't do it. Just make sure that you tell him or her in a loving way that you aren't comfortable with that suggestion, and explain that your discomfort is not a reflection of your love.

But if it's something you feel is not wrong but merely different, you might consider experimenting a little. There can be a fine line between wrong and creative, so think—and pray—carefully about your decision.

Think back to the Song of Solomon. The couple in that book was enjoying each other's body! And that was God's original idea. The important point is that you and your spouse are expressing love for each other. Don't be afraid that you're doing something wrong just because you make love in a different position, for example.

A special word is in order here regarding pornography: The enemy loves to take something beautiful and turn it into something more useful for his own evil kingdom. You should know that it is neither healthy nor normal for anyone, man or woman, to need pornographic input to create the atmosphere for sexual activity. If this applies to you (or your spouse), please seek professional Christian counsel. From the attorney general's report with which Dr. James Dobson was involved in 1986, I've learned that the stuff that's out there today isn't the typical bare-breast material that captivated my schoolmates a few decades ago. Today, truly vile junk is readily available. I'm typing this section as rapidly as I can because I don't like remembering some of the sections from the attorney general's report. In fact, when I was assigned to read it as an editor in New York, I had to repeatedly whisper the name of Jesus to wash out my brain afterward.

Men go into a "coma" after they make love
Lots of women complain that their husband turns over and starts snoring as soon as they've made love. Women, men can't help it—physiologically, they're exhausted. So if he immediately drops off to sleep, please don't take it as a personal rejection. One young husband explained men's "passing out" this way: "We're enjoying the fact that we don't have to think about sex for the next five minutes."

And men, try *not* to fall asleep immediately. Or if you're prone (pun!) to do that, at least wrap your arms around your wife. Otherwise, it's easy for her to feel used.

HOW IMPORTANT IS YOUR MARRIAGE?
If things are a bit sluggish right now, how do you renew that loving feeling? It starts with basic trust—trust that you both want to work on this area of your life and that you aren't ready to throw in the

towel yet. But it takes time—and the determination that this is important to you both. In other words, you have to put your marriage first. For many wives, that means they must determine to see their husband through different eyes—eyes of appreciation.

I remember one retreat where I was encouraging the women to be interested in whatever interested their husband. I even told how I'd read the sports page each day so I could discuss issues that Don liked. (I also confessed that while I desperately miss my husband, I don't miss football one bit!) But because he liked to have me watch the games with him, I did. I quilted or thumbed through catalogs or wrote letters, but I was there. And I cheered when he cheered and groaned when he groaned and never once asked, "Who's playing again?"

Was that being deceptive? Not at all. I didn't love football—and Don knew it—but I did love my husband. And if he enjoyed having me watch the game with him while the kids were napping, then that's what I wanted to do. After all, I knew there were plenty of other women out there who would be happy to watch football with him. And when I make that point at retreats, I get plenty of nods in response.

But let me back up a bit and tell about one particular retreat. After one of my sessions, a woman in a blue sweater stopped by my cabin to talk about her feelings for another woman's husband. I got right to the point: "Are you involved sexually?"

"No," she answered, then added softly, "not yet."

As my eyebrows arched, she said quickly, "But you don't understand how awful his wife is to him. He really is a sweet, loving man, but nothing he does ever pleases her, and she always puts him down in public."

I heard her out for almost an hour but reminded her that she was playing with fire that was about to destroy a family, tarnish her own life, and ripple out to others in the church. As I prayed with her, I asked God to strengthen her and help her seek his face and hear his voice only.

She thanked me, and as she left she added, "I wouldn't stand a chance if she'd just be kind to him." I've heard the his-wife-just-doesn't-understand-him line so much that I just shook my head and wrapped another prayer around her.

Then in the evening session, I talked about the importance of being interested in things our husbands are interested in, concluding with my typical line: "So, if it's important to your husband to have you watch football with him, do that. After all, there are plenty of other women out there who would be only too happy to watch with him."

As usual, several women nodded, but one woman to my right snorted, "Not my husband!" and laughed. I was startled that she would say that publicly, even as a joke. The line did get a good laugh, and while I waited for the group to settle down, a woman in a blue sweater caught my eye and gave me a see-I-told-you-so look. *Oh!* She was the one who had confessed her love for another's husband. She hadn't been making up the wife's disrespect after all.

I often wonder how that situation finally played itself out, but I'm afraid to dwell on the details since I'm convinced it ended in greater pain.

WATCH YOUR THOUGHTS

This business of the thought life is very important. Remember the old saying, "Sow a thought, reap an action. Sow an action, reap a habit. Sow a habit, reap a character. Sow a character, reap a destiny"? Yes, that first wicked thought is where we fight the battle, not later on when we're in bed with someone else's spouse.

Years ago, one of my dear friends started helping a young woman in his office with her boyfriend problems. It felt good to be needed by someone who thanked him with such a beautiful smile whenever he stopped by her desk—and it didn't hurt that she was so pretty, either. Soon he found himself whistling more as he dressed for work in the morning. And he noticed that his grooming habits had perked up, too.

That would have been the time to grab himself by the shoulders and say, "Stop it. Don't pretend you don't know where this is leading. You're wondering if you've still got it, so spend more time with your wife. Stop this!"

But he didn't have that little talk with himself and instead kept fooling himself. (Often, the biggest lies we tell are the ones we tell ourselves.) Soon he and this young lady were having lunch a couple of times a week, just as "friends"—or so he would have said. Then one day, they stopped by the lake to look at the fall colors before going back to the office, and he put his arm around her as he directed her attention to a flock of geese. Next thing you know, they were, as he later sadly said, "necking like a couple of teenagers." Within a matter of days, they were involved in a full-fledged affair that ultimately destroyed their reputations and cost him his family and his leadership role in the church.

I have a counselor friend who tells pastors to cancel any appointment that they're looking forward to. He's had too many clergy destroy their marriages, families, and ministries just because they've started out counseling a member of their congregation and had it turn into a full-blown affair—with each party saying, "But we never meant this to happen."

TRANSFERENCE

Before we leave this subject, I want to comment on the occurrence of being drawn to someone wonderful—a pastor, a coworker, or a kind neighbor. This situation is so common it even has a name: transference. All the energy and attention that had previously been directed to a spouse is now directed toward someone who is not an appropriate recipient. And there's a sneaky thing that happens in the midst of trauma: Someone who is hurting will look to another he or she respects and, all too soon, can get caught up in a bad situation—especially if the other person is experiencing marital tension, too. This is a fallen world; even those who want to follow the Lord sometimes indulge in some pretty stupid thought processes that tempt us to look to another to fill emotional needs that should be filled only by our spouse. That's thin ice that no one should tread on.

But if you're already on that thin ice, don't rationalize it by saying, "Well, I've already sinned in my heart, and Jesus said that's the same as doing it, so I might as well go ahead and commit the act." That's the height of stupid rationalization.

In Matthew 5:28, he says, "But I say, anyone who even looks at a woman with lust in his eye has already committed adultery with her in his heart."

Don't stop there; go on to verses 29-30: "So if your eye—even if it is your good eye—causes you to lust, gouge it out and throw it away. It is better for you to lose one part of your body than for your whole body to be thrown into hell. And if your hand—even if it is your stronger hand—causes you to sin, cut it off and throw it away. It is better for you to lose one part of your body than for your whole body to be thrown into hell."

After reading those last two verses, which allude to what should happen to eyes that might look or hands that might touch sinfully, do you still think it's all right to go through with the sexual act and lose *that* part of your body?

Jesus said that if a man lusts, he has committed the sin because that's where the action starts—in the thought. If you deal with the thought, then you need confess only to God. But if you carry out the thought, more lives will be involved—and ultimately destroyed.

And for crying out loud, don't go to the person you've been thinking about and ask him or her to pray that you'll be able to conquer your lustful thoughts. That's going to grab the attention of most people and light a dangerous emotional fire. Just deal with it with the Lord and perhaps with a trusted Christian friend of the same gender. You'll have fewer regrets that way.

One of the pastors in our Michigan town used that ploy to his advantage. He was one of those outgoing types who won the trust of several hurting women in his congregation. Later we found out that he had more than just their trust. And his mode of operation was to "confess" to a woman that he wanted her to pray for him about his wrong thoughts toward her. Later, he'd invite her to his study so they could pray together. Bingo. Apparently, years before, he had been sincere, although foolish, in his confession to a woman in his first congregation. Once he learned the results of such an action, he proceeded to use it often.

Guard your heart, and keep your marriage bed pure. And when those lackluster moments come, think back to those days of early dating when the excitement was new and shiny. What can you do to bring back those feelings? Often it starts with the little things. One gal suggested they neck in the drive when they got home from church one night. Be creative!

And don't ever think you're too old for this stuff. One of the relatives once asked my seventy-five-year-old grandfather at what age men begin to slow down sexually. Papa looked up from the pile of wood he was stacking and grinned. "You'll have to ask someone a lot older than me!"

Whew! Now, if you'll excuse me, I think I'll work on the budget chapter. Either that or go put a load of wash in the machine—in *cold* water.

SIMPLE REMINDERS

1. Sexual intercourse was God's idea. It's our enemy, Satan, who has distorted what was a great idea and tried to use it for his own evil purposes.

2. For women, great sex starts long before bedtime.
3. Turn off the TV, and turn on your mate.
4. Love is spelled T-I-M-E. If your busy schedule demands that something has to go, make sure it isn't your sexual relationship.
5. Don't compare your wife to another woman.
6. Children will change the relationship, so make the necessary adjustments.
7. Don't take it personally if your husband goes into a "coma" after making love.
8. Don't take one another for granted—ever.
9. Guard your heart, and keep the marriage bed pure.
10. Don't ever think you're "too old" for that stuff.

DISCUSSION QUESTIONS

1. What advice do you wish someone had given you about the sexual side of marriage?
2. What's the greatest challenge to keeping the spark alive in your marriage?
3. If you have children, what adjustments have you made?
4. How have you handled temptation?
5. What advice would you give couples just starting out?

CHAPTER 4

Husbands Don't Have Scriptwriters

IN Colorado, the TV program *Dr. Quinn: Medicine Woman* is very popular, especially among college women. Holly and her friends all watch it. If they're out for the evening, they tape it. If they're home, they unplug the phone. Even moms are not allowed to call during that time. This is serious stuff. And they all sigh over the character Sully, who is strong and sensitive and who, in addition to being good looking, always knows the right thing to say in any critical moment.

Holly was watching it at home one weekend and sighing every time Sully did something wonderful, which was quite often. After one of Holly's quiet heaves, I glanced at her and decided Sully's character was not good for my daughter's thought life. Then I looked back at the screen just as Sully stood behind Dr. Quinn, with his hands protectively on her shoulders, and realized that man wasn't good for *my* thought life.

I waited for the commercial before offering my dose of reality: "Holly, do you think women all over the nation are sighing when they watch this?"

She smiled. "Ohhhhh, yeah."

"Well, that concerns me because Sully isn't real," I said. "He has a scriptwriter! In fact, he probably has *twelve* of them. That means that good husbands all over the United States are being compared to a perfect character right now, and they're coming up short in their wives' minds. . . . Remember that when your future husband doesn't always do the 'right' thing. He won't have a scriptwriter, either."

Amazingly, she didn't roll her eyes at my impromptu lecture. Good for her. Unfortunately, many young couples have seen more TV sitcoms than real-life examples of godly marriages, so they don't have a clue that a solid relationship requires commitment first and hard work second. Young marrieds shouldn't expect their spouses to have scriptwriters who will ensure that all problems are solved in fifty-one minutes or less.

WATCHING OTHERS

Think of this Sunday morning scenario: You're on your way to church—and for the entire drive, the two of you are complaining to one another. He gripes about your not being ready on time and says, "Every Sunday we go through this!"

And you respond, "Well, if you'd help instead of sitting out in the driveway and racing the motor . . ."

And that verbal sniping continues until you pull into the parking lot, get out of the car, and with all sweetness greet your coworshipers: "Goooood morning."

The problem is, you've parked next to the blue Chevrolet belonging to John and Mary. John gets out and goes around to the other side and opens the car door for Mary.

Now you and your husband are walking into church. You may even take his arm, not because you're overwhelmed with love for the man right at that moment, but because you have something to say.

And what you say is, "Did you see how *John* got out and opened the car door?"

The not-so-subtle implication is that John treats *his* wife better than *your* husband treats his.

What you don't know is that John *had* to open the car door because Mary's sitting there saying, "I ain't gettin' out!"

Meanwhile, John and Mary are walking behind you. And Mary hisses into John's ear, "Do you see how they walk so close? Now *there's* a couple who's still in love!"

We don't dare think that we know what goes on in another's heart—or home. Karen was helping in the church kitchen one night when Lynn, the second wife of one of the deacons, brought her potluck dish in to be reheated. After Lynn left, one of the other workers turned to Karen and babbled, "Now there's a match made in heaven! I've never known such a happy family. Isn't it wonderful how the Lord brought them together after their first spouses died? They're soooo much in love."

Karen smiled and quickly busied herself at the sink. She and her husband often socialized with the couple and knew the truth: Both deeply regretted the marriage, resented the other's children, and wondered where their heads had been when they decided to get married.

When are we going to stop comparing our marriages to others'—and deciding theirs are better?

All of us can be perfect—for about two seconds a day. The problems come when we catch others in those two seconds and think they are always like that. So we go through life trying to live up to unrealistic expectations and heaping tension upon our spouses because everything isn't always ideal. Remember, no one can sprint a marathon, and since marital commitment is for the long haul, we might as well relax and enjoy the view along the way.

A DOSE OF REALITY

I love it that when the Lord said, "Come unto me," he *didn't* say, "Come with a right attitude" or "Come with a smile on your face" or even "Come without tears." He just said, "Come!" So talk to him about the frustrations you face in your relationship with your mate.

What if we determined every day to stop expecting our non-scripted spouse to be all that we need and started encouraging him or her instead?

We need godly examples

So many men and women today haven't had godly examples within their own young lives, so they don't know how to do this "marriage thing." They have the Bible as a guide, of course, but they need older couples to translate those godly principles and show them how to do it right. Some churches have a mentoring class that matches successful older couples with younger ones—befriending them and loving them through the crises.

Such an arrangement proved to be the lifeline that Eric and Belinda needed when they disagreed about where to live. Belinda had grown up in a family that moved often, always living in run-down apartments. To her, security meant a house—complete with a white picket fence—and she wanted it *now*. Eric, on the other hand, wanted to stay in their apartment for at least another year so they could investigate the various areas in town and save a greater amount for that future down payment. He heard Belinda's pleas as nagging and tuned her out. That, in turn, made her all the more frightened that she would never have the security that had eluded her during childhood.

Then one Saturday morning over coffee with their new mentoring friends, Clyde and Grace, the housing issue came up. Within a few minutes, the older couple had gotten to the root issue of the disagreement—the younger couple's differing sense of security—and shared a little about their own early disagreements. When they parted that day, both couples were happier—Clyde and Grace because they had made a difference in another couple's marriage and Eric and Belinda because they had a new understanding of the dynamics that drove each other.

Men need respect

Of course, women need respect, too, but this is an especially critical area for a man. And respecting your husband starts with refusing to compare him to another man—TV character or not. I remember one frustrating morning when Don made several trips to our local hardware store to get the proper gizmo to hook up our dryer. By the third trip, he was starting to call himself names, saying any "dummy" should be able to do this. I could have confirmed his inability and suggested that he call John, a friend who could do anything, or even call a professional repairman, but I knew this job had grown into a personal challenge.

"Donnie, you're not dumb!" I said. "Dummies wouldn't even know what part to ask for. Sure, you don't do this stuff for a living, but I know you can do it. Actually, I think you just like going to the hardware store to check out that new blonde cashier. She is a cutie, isn't she?"

He grinned, made a final trip to the store, and finished the chore by lunchtime.

But what if he hadn't been able to do the job and needed to call in the repairman? That would have been the time to remind him that he could do things that other husbands couldn't, including putting up with me—a statement that always brought a quick smile to his face—and filling out the tax forms and calming down hotheaded relatives. The main thing is to help your guy concentrate on his personal worth—as a husband and a man.

Men need space

Often when we women are troubled, we want to call in our personal troops to help us work through the situation and settle on a quick solution. But often a man needs to be alone to work through the alternatives. So let him have his space. If you'll give him that time alone, he'll come back. But we mustn't follow him into the garage and then back into the house and then out to the mailbox, all the while whining, "What's wrong? What have I done?"

A better route is to acknowledge that you recognize that he's upset, ask if you've done anything wrong, and if so, how you can fix it. Ask if he wants to talk about it. And if not, then let him know that you're available if he wants to talk later, and leave him alone. I wish I'd known earlier that men as a rule don't like to be bugged. I saved both of us much grief when I finally figured out that Don needed to process a situation before he could comfortably discuss it with me.

Men need trust

With great sadness, I remember a young sailor husband who was trying to live a godly life while away but was surrounded by worldly shipmates who accepted every temptation whenever they put into port. He needed encouragement and trust from his wife, but her cousin continually taunted her with stories of his own wicked choices in those same ports, adding gleeful comments like, "He's probably at that little pink house right now!"

Rather than reassuring her husband of her love and her trust in his good decisions, this wife turned every phone call into a tirade of accusations about where he had undoubtedly been. He was thousands of miles from home, terribly lonely, and feeling as though he was fighting a losing battle.

What a gift his wife could have given him if she had stressed her trust in him, first to her cousin and then to her husband! But out of her fear, she listened to someone who projected his own actions onto another. Sadly, that marriage didn't survive.

Men need acceptance

We women are great "fixers," since we've been trained that way from childhood. But our men don't want us to fix *them*. (They need a wife, not another mother.) Somebody out there just thought, *But it's difficult to stand by and watch him do it wrong.* Hmmm. Let's talk about that concept of "wrong." Of course, we think of major areas such as job choice and clothes preference when we talk about acceptance, and every women's magazine has presented the importance of surrounding our mate with that feeling that his esteem is safe when he's with his wife. So let's talk about something more troublesome: folding towels. Every woman seems to have a particular way that she likes (insists upon) having the bath towels folded. If her husband doesn't do it right, she may just insist upon doing it herself. And most men are only too glad to let her.

If you choose that route, make sure you don't grumble later about never getting any help. You must be patient and loving—and willing to accept less than your standard of perfection. Think about it. Does it really matter if the towels are folded with the edges tucked in as opposed to a once-over fold? Isn't the important thing to have them folded? You may be saying, "But it's just as easy to fold them twice as to fold them once. So why can't he just do it right?"

My newly married friend Kathy recently told me about the disagreement she and her husband had about doing the laundry. Both of them had lived on their own for several years before they got married, so they both had pretty well-developed methods for washing clothes.

But a problem arose since Timothy had no experience with the special laundering instructions many women's clothes have. Kathy found that often things were wrinkled that wouldn't have been wrinkled if *she* had washed them, and once he ran her nylons and bras through the dryer when they should have been hung up to dry. Even though he was nice enough to help out with the laundry, he didn't meet Kathy's expectations for how it should have been done.

Kathy realized that, as I've tried to explain, her relationship with her husband was much more important than the state of her clothes. It wasn't going to kill her if a few things were wrinkled or even if a pair of nylons got ruined, for that matter! She thought she had adjusted her attitude sufficiently, until one Saturday morning.

That day Kathy was doing the laundry, and Timothy, being in the basement at the time, started the water running into the washer to give her a head start. But by the time she got downstairs and sorted out the next load, the whole washer was full of water. She was really ticked at the idea of shoving her clothes down into the water, and she made him come down and do it himself. That sort of brought to a head all of Kathy's frustration about the issue, so she decided to talk to Timothy about the whole laundry situation.

Timothy was justifiably angry that his wife was so mad about something so inconsequential *and* his attempt to help her out, at that. They finally decided that they should still take turns doing the laundry, but since he didn't know how her various things needed to be washed, she would sort them out and give him any special instructions before he started. But once either of them got started, the other should stay out of it and avoid trying to help—since they recognized that they had different methods that were equally valid but not especially compatible!

Personally, I think it's rather pathetic when a wife puts her need to control—to have it done the "right" way—ahead of her husband's self-esteem. Of course, if he's trying to please you, he'll eventually catch on to how you want those dumb towels folded and how to launder your undies. But in the meantime, lighten up.

We all need appreciation
Saying "Thank you—I really appreciate your help" goes a long way toward making your spouse want to jump in and help the next time. And an honest "I loved the way you handled Josh. Your calmness helped him get a handle on his temper and set the mood for the entire meeting" will surround him or her for days—and help produce that needed calmness again. Face it, we all want to know that our efforts are noticed—and appreciated.

I love the story of the ringmaster who was challenged by a grumpy window washer: "How come you circus people always need applause?" he asked. "I wash windows all week long, and nobody applauds me."

The ringmaster smiled. "Ah, but think how it would change your job if they did applaud!"

How would a little verbal applause change your relationship? Men, especially, need adoration. OK, husbands undoubtedly are never going to say, "I need you to adore me a little," but try it occasionally anyway and see what happens. Oh, *not* a "My, my, but aren't you just the biggest, strongest man on earth?!" but a sincere recognition of his efforts and abilities.

My New York friends Tim and Louann, a young couple with two small children, were vacationing nearby so they stopped in for dinner recently. As we caught up on the lives of mutual friends, Louann mentioned one couple who had married four years ago. Shaking her head, she added, "Glenda just adores Philip." She said it with mild disgust, but I caught the look on Tim's face—one of bewildered longing. It was as though he was thinking, *I wish you'd adore me.* And maybe some honest adoration was exactly what their relationship needed.

At couples' retreats, I've dared to say, "Women, if you want to be treated more like a queen, try treating your man like a king." Some of the women glare at me, but the men always nod. We're all looking for a harbor in this pitiful world—a place where we know we are safe and loved and appreciated and even adored a little. Let's work on providing that for each other.

Recognize that men and women do not think alike
Remember the song "Why Can't a Woman Be More like a Man?" from *My Fair Lady*? Professor Higgins was frustrated that his student, a woman, was thinking like a *woman* instead of like a man! We chuckle, but more than once I've listened to young wives

wanting their husbands to think like women. It amazes me that we marry someone precisely because his characteristics fill in those missing from our lives, and then we spend the rest of our life trying to change that person.

I'm fortunate to have learned early that men and women are different—and I learned that in the tiny Four Mile Missionary Baptist Church on the banks of the Cumberland River in Harlan County, Kentucky. The women and children sat on the left side of the church, while the men sat on the right side (probably so their wives couldn't nudge them awake during the sermon!). At the time, I never questioned the situation; that's just the way things were. Allow me to pause here, as I revel in the memories of a June evening breeze and sounds of the tree frogs floating through the open windows. A tall, dark-haired mountaineer sat in the back each Sunday evening and, in his bass voice, led us by lining the songs— singing one line at a time, then waiting for the congregation to sing it after him. Even now I can hear him: "Life's evening sun (and we'd repeat) . . . is sinking low (we'd repeat). A few more days . . . and I must go. . . ." I'd gladly go back to having men and women sitting on opposite sides of the church if that childhood sense of security would come with it.

Jay and Holly taught me further that men and women are as different as night and day—even when they're raised in the same home by the same parents. Three months after we moved to Colorado, they flew back to see their New York friends perform in a school play at the old high school. They flew out on the same morning, but because of their friends' schedules, they made arrangements to fly home on separate days. (By the way, Jay will not sit with Holly on a plane. For those of you who have children in this stage, please don't think they love each other any less just because they don't want to be seen together in public. Jay will not sit with his sister nor acknowledge her, but I've noticed that he watches her like a hawk, and nobody better mess with her.)

I pickcd up Holly at the airport in Denver on Wednesday. She got off the plane, hugged me, and started talking. She talked for an hour and fifteen minutes! She and Jay had attended our old New York church that past Sunday, so I heard who had changed their hairstyle, who had gotten married, who was divorced, who was pregnant, who'd had a baby, what the baby weighed at birth, what its name was, and what the mother dressed it in for church. I even heard about the pastor's tie. She talked nonstop until we walked into our home, where the phone was ringing. The call was for Holly.

The next day I went to the airport to pick up Jay. He got off the plane, hugged me, and said, "Hi, Ma. Everybody you ever met in New York says hi." End of discussion. He didn't say another word. He read all the way home to Colorado Springs.

I say all that to encourage you wives to stop expecting the men in your life to respond the way your dear female friend or daughter would. And wives and husbands both need to stop expecting their spouse to follow an unwritten script for how a husband or wife *should* respond. Start showing appreciation for who your mate is right now. And then stand back and watch the good things that will happen.

SIMPLE REMINDERS

1. Husbands shouldn't be expected to respond to a situation in the same way that a TV character—who has twelve scriptwriters—would respond.
2. Many young couples have seen more TV sitcoms than real-life examples of godly marriages, so they don't have a clue that a solid relationship requires commitment first and hard work second.
3. All of us can be perfect—for about two seconds a day.

4. We don't dare think that we know what goes on in another's heart—or home.

5. No one can sprint a marathon, and since marital commitment is for the long haul, we might as well relax and enjoy the view along the way.

6. When the Lord said, "Come unto me," he *didn't* add, "but come with a smile on your face." So talk to him about the frustrations you have in your marriage.

7. We need godly examples in order to do marriage "right."

8. Men need respect.

9. Let the three *A*'s guide your relationship: acceptance, appreciation, and adoration.

10. Recognize that men and women do not think alike.

DISCUSSION QUESTIONS

1. What are some of the problems you encounter when you compare your spouse to a TV character?

2. Have you and your spouse been mentored by an older couple? If so, what was the situation?

3. What situation opened your eyes to the fact that men and women do not think alike?

4. How did each of you respond? What was the result?

5. What do you wish someone had told you early in your marriage about respect for your spouse?

6. How have you shown acceptance, appreciation, and/or adoration for each other? What were the results?

CHAPTER 5

Men Read Newspapers, Not Minds

OR fifteen years, I taught college preparatory classes in a Detroit area high school and often gave essay tests. After I'd give only partial credit for an incomplete answer, a student would invariably ask, "Why'd you take off four points? You know what I meant." My retort was always the same: "No, I read papers; I don't read minds."

And that's a good reminder for any wife who expects her husband to know intuitively what she wants him to do. It took Marcie a couple of disappointments to catch on to that concept. She enjoyed strolling through antique malls, and if she found a piece of Nippon for her knickknack shelf, all the better. But her frustration was that she would have liked her husband, Mark, along for company. She never asked him to go, but she'd get angry when he didn't offer.

She'd carry on arguments in her mind with him: *I go to the car lots with you, but will you go to an antique shop with me? Nooo! But if one of your buddies wanted you to go someplace, you'd be out the door before he finished hanging up the phone!*

One day, she argued so much in her mind that she finally said aloud to Mark, "It really irritates me that you don't want to go to the antique mall with me!"

He looked around, as though wondering where in the world that comment came from. Then he calmly said, "I didn't know you'd like me to go. You never said anything, so I assumed you liked having that time to yourself."

Now it was her turn to be surprised. "Well, you should have known I'd like you along!"

"Now, Marcie, how could I have known that?" he asked. "As much as I love you, I can't read your mind."

Marcie gave an exasperated huff. "All right. Would you like to go to the mall with me?"

Mark grinned. "I'd love to, honey. Thanks for letting me know."

A SIMPLE SOLUTION

Let's face it, wives. Hinting, pouting, and sighing simply won't get you the desired results. You have to ask clearly. In fact, most men are such "bottom line" thinkers that you may actually have to spell it out. When I taught high schoolers persuasive speaking, I suggested they use a three-part outline: Problem, Cause, Solution. Wouldn't that practice work in a marriage? What if you said, "I'm feeling overwhelmed (Problem) by numerous demands on my schedule (Cause), and I want to hire a cleaning lady one day a week" (Solution)?

Now, true, your husband may disagree and offer other solutions, but at least he's not feeling personally attacked—as in "You never help around here. I'm going to hire a cleaning lady." I'm convinced that such clear communication can do wonders.

When I worked in New York for a Christian magazine, I often had the opportunity to do home visitation with Delia Garcia, one of our association's family specialists. One afternoon, we were in the Bronx apartment of a family in crisis. The wife had called, saying between sobs that she had finally faced the fact that her marriage was over. She wanted help with bus tickets for herself and the couple's two young children to go back to her family.

Soon Delia and I were in the family's tiny apartment, perched on unsteady kitchen chairs. The wife sat on the faded sofa, holding a silent, wide-eyed little girl of about two. Their son, perhaps five, leaned against her. The husband opened a lawn chair for himself and sat with his arms folded defiantly, but with a bewildered expression on his face.

We chatted about general things—how the son was doing in kindergarten, how the couple had met, the father's job with the sanitation department. Then Delia got to the point: "We understand you're having trouble in your marriage. Would you like to tell us about it?"

The husband shrugged and looked toward his wife. She pulled the little girl closer and said quietly, "Our marriage is over. I love him, but he doesn't love me anymore."

He frowned at her and shook his head as he turned back to Delia and said, "I work hard. I even take overtime so she doesn't have to get a job and can stay with our children. On Sunday afternoons, so she and the baby can rest, I take the boy with me to the dump to shoot rats. How can she say I don't love her?" He shrugged again.

Delia turned back to the wife and asked, "Why *do* you think he doesn't love you?"

Tears welled up in the woman's dark eyes. "He comes home, fills his dinner plate with whatever I have on the stove, and goes into the bedroom and turns on the TV. He never eats with us."

The husband was staring at his wife with the most dumbfounded expression I'd ever seen. Then he turned to Delia and said, "I come home dirty, I fill my plate, I take a quick shower, and I eat while I watch the news."

Delia smiled. "Would it be possible for you to do all that except eating? Then after the news, you could have dinner with your family instead of eating alone in the bedroom."

He frowned, then looked back at his tearful wife. "OK. I can do that. I didn't know it was such a big deal."

CREATIVE NUMBERS

Communication is vital for any husband and wife who care about their relationship. And it's not only men who have a hard time knowing what their spouse wants. Just ask Aggie.

She and Ernest were both older when they married—and a little set in their ways. Complicating their communication challenge was Ernest's timid nature and the fact that his first language was not English. Aggie had a tendency not to notice Ernest's comments because of his offhanded way of presenting them. And when she did notice what he said, she was never sure if she was understanding how he really felt.

Then one May morning, a graduation announcement arrived from his nephew several states away. In Aggie's own large extended family, such events were pleas for the customary check, but Ernest casually mentioned that he'd like to attend.

"Oh, just send a card," was her quick comment.

Ernest nodded and turned to go into the garage, but something in his gentle resignation caught Aggie's attention. As she pondered the dilemma, she turned the announcement envelope over and drew a chart—five squares in a row, numbered from one to five. Then she labeled each square: One meant "I really don't want to do this." Two was "I don't want to do this, but I'm willing to talk about it." Three equalled "I don't care one way or another." Four stood for "I'd like to do this, but I won't die if we don't." And five announced "Yes, this is very, very important to me."

Then she took the chart to Ernest, explained the numbers, and asked him how he would rate his nephew's graduation.

To her surprise, Ernest pointed to the five and said, "He's that important."

Aggie had met this family at the wedding and remembered that even though their English was flawless, they spoke to Ernest only in their own language even in her presence. Now *she* had a decision: Would she accompany Ernest to the graduation?

Turning to the chart again, Aggie asked how badly Ernest wanted her to accompany him. He thought for a moment and then said, "A four. Yes, a four. I'd like you to be there, but I'll understand if you don't want to go."

Then, having caught on to this new way of communicating, he said, "What number would you choose?"

As thoughts of the long drive collided with Aggie's concern that the family wouldn't speak English, her first impulse was to choose number one—the "I really don't want to do this" response. But if this event was so important to Ernest, perhaps she ought to be open to discussing it. Thus, she chose number two—the "but I'm willing to talk about it" category.

As they talked, Aggie explained her dismay at the thought of a six-hundred-mile trip in one day—which was Ernest's usual way of traveling. To her surprise, he nodded, then said, "We could leave a day early, drive until midafternoon, and find a nice place to stay. Then the next morning, we'll have a late breakfast and arrive at my brother's at the time he would normally expect us."

With that hurdle behind her, Aggie then presented her concern that his family left her out of conversations by speaking their own language.

Ernest's eyes widened. "Oh, we don't mean to be rude. We get excited to talk, and they know that my English doesn't keep up with my thoughts. We'll do better."

So the arrangements were made, and to Aggie's surprise, the trip was wonderful. Not only was it leisurely, but since Aggie now understood that Ernest felt inadequate to express himself well in English, she was more tolerant of his lapsing back into his own language. And she had an ally in her fifteen-year-old niece, Sabrina, who enjoyed translating for Aggie. That good bonding time would never have happened if Aggie hadn't come up with a better way to communicate with her husband.

59

LOVE LANGUAGES

I wish I had known earlier that spouses hear "I love you" in different ways. I didn't know that there are actually five languages of love: words, gifts, touch, acts of service, and quality time.

I first heard this concept when Dr. Gary Chapman, a Winston-Salem pastor and counselor, spoke at Maranatha Bible and Missionary Conference in Muskegon, Michigan, several years ago.[1] He had my attention as soon as he said that we hear expressions of love in different ways and that, invariably, a husband and wife do not have the same love language. Then he listed five languages:

Words

Folks who have the language of words need to hear things like "I love you," "Thank you," "I'm glad you're part of our family," "I'm so glad I married you."

As I listened to Dr. Chapman, I nodded. With my straightforward manner, I identified with those who want the clear-cut direction words give.

Gifts

To those who have this language, a gift says, "I was thinking of you when I saw this on my trip." Are you always buying gifts for someone else, and you don't understand why she never buys you gifts? All she wants to do is go out for dinner every few weeks and chat? She's into "quality time."

Quality time

These folks see the hours spent together as a special expression of love. When I heard this, I suddenly understood why the men in my family insist that their wives go fishing with them all day—they're quality-time people.

Touch

Dr. Chapman said husbands understand this one best, but feel as though their wives often say, "No touch without the words." But touch doesn't have to be limited to the sexual act. Even our teens who are too "grown-up" to be hugged will appreciate a pat on the back when we go past them. And a son who has had a rough day will know by your grip on his shoulder that you care.

Acts of service

Those of us who respond to acts of service say, "Don't *talk* about love; show me."

I remember one Saturday when I was running late for a meeting at church and then discovered that my car had a flat tire. Don insisted that I take his car so I wouldn't be late. When I pulled into the drive two hours later, he had not only changed my tire, but he was just finishing washing and waxing my car. Boy, that spoke volumes of love to me.

When my teens and I heard Dr. Chapman's observations, Jay suddenly turned to me and said, "You're acts of service!"

I nodded. "You got it."

He leaned closer and whispered, "I always wondered why you'd get so ticked when I wouldn't clean my room."

You see, Jay is quality time. He liked spending time with me even then, but he didn't get excited about cleaning up his room since it just got messy again. If he could walk from the door to his bed, it was clean enough. Now he realized that the fact that he didn't clean his room made me think, *Jay, you don't love me*.

But he wasn't saying that at all! In fact, he was saying that he *did* love me when he spent time with me and just hung out with me.

As you apply this idea to marriage, you need to know that people tend to express love the way they'd like to be loved. Kari spent several hours thinking up three pages of activities to offer her husband for his birthday. He wasn't impressed; he just wanted to spend a quiet day at home reading the World War II historical novel he'd found at a garage sale several weeks before. She was hurt because he so easily dismissed something she had put a lot of time into. She would have loved it if he had custom-made a gift like that for her. But that was the whole point: She gave something that she would have loved rather than giving him what he wanted. It's important to understand which languages you and your spouse favor, both so that you can express love in the way it is most likely to be understood and so that you can "hear" your spouse's expressions of love even though they may differ from what you are looking for.

WOMEN NEED WOMEN

Dr. James Dobson says, "Research makes it clear that little girls are blessed with greater linguistic ability than little boys, and it remains a lifelong talent. Simply stated, she talks more than he. As an adult . . . God may have given her 50,000 words per day and her husband only 25,000. He comes home from work with 24,975 used up and merely grunts his way through the evening. He may descend into Monday Night Football while his wife is dying to expend her remaining 25,000 words."[2]

We women want to talk in great detail, but our men don't want the details. Here's an example: After you go to your favorite restaurant with your friend Nena and your husband asks, "How was dinner?" he wants to hear, "Nena and I had a great talk. Thank you for staying with the children. I really appreciate that."

Unless he asks more questions, that's all he wants to hear. Do not say, "It was wonderful. But when we got there we had to wait a while because the waitress dropped a tray of glasses, and they were trying to sweep them up. But finally Nena and I got a table, but remember how I always like to order grilled chicken with sprouts? Well, they were out of the sprouts, and then they had to substitute the sourdough bread instead of the whole wheat bread. You know, your mother promised that she was going to give me that sourdough recipe, and she just never did. . . ." Believe me, he doesn't want to hear it.

Watch children play. The girls talk and play in relationship ways. They're directing: "No, do it this way." They're supporting: "That's right. Put them over here."

But boys—and men—relate to each other through activities. They play team sports, they go golfing, they work on something together. For the most part, guys don't go out just to talk. I think of the Monday Night Football games Don and his buddies watched together, which I thought were a waste of time. I was much more interested in getting together with "the girls" and catching up on all of the personal news.

We women need one another—not only to encourage each other but also to talk to each other. A husband cannot be all a wife needs. And she can't be all that he needs, either. A good relationship means we enjoy spending time together, yes, but it also expands to include other friendships and other projects.

Let's face it—for the most part, men don't know that when we wives have a problem, we do *not* want to hear solutions. We want to vent and be hugged.

Teri's day at the real estate office had been horrid. First her car wouldn't start, then two clients canceled, then the lockbox wouldn't yield at another house a third client had really wanted to see. When she got home, Fred started with his usual "Well, did you . . . ?" But this time, Teri had the good sense to look at him and say, "Fred, I don't want advice, I want sympathy. An 'oh, poor dear' will go a long way right about now."

Fred wrapped his arms around her and in his best Southern accent said, "Oh, my poor hard-workin' little darlin.' I'm sorry you had such a rotten day. Just let me rub your tired shoulders while you tell me about all those bad people."

It was just funny enough to make her smile, which in itself helped relieve the tension.

MAN TO MAN

One activity that Don and I both enjoyed was a Bible study with several other couples from our Sunday school class. There we could concentrate on an activity while getting to know other couples on a deeper level. To the wives' delight, the men gradually learned that they enjoyed having other men with whom to discuss important family issues. And out of those discussions came the insight that they weren't alone in learning how to deal with these creatures they'd married.

That Bible study was a form of the now popular "accountability group," which is just a fancy term for friends getting together and asking each other how things are really going. One of my favorite Dutchmen, Morrie Driesenga, leads a Wednesday morning men's group in Holland, Michigan. When he first came to the Lord, he says it was the quiet encouragement and warm handshakes from other men that helped keep him on track and made him want to know more about the Lord. The men's group grew out of a coffee meeting with his pastor when Morrie asked, "What can you teach me about prayer?" Within a few weeks, Morrie began meeting with the pastor and two other men every Wednesday for breakfast. From there, the group expanded as more men were drawn into the friendship circle.

Now each week they begin the session with Scripture, and the week's leader asks individuals how the group can best pray for them. That makes it easy for the men to open up about what's going on in their lives. Many groups limit the size so it doesn't become too large, with men feeling left out and not having a chance to share. A few of the groups that I know about start with a passage of Scripture or a verse that everyone was asked to memorize and ponder during the previous week. Then each person takes a turn answering several key questions: How was your week? How are you doing with God? with your wife? (or, for the unmarried man, with the woman you're dating?) with your children? What temptations are you facing? How are you doing there? How was your thought life this week? Are you spending time in the Word and in prayer? How can we pray for you?

Many men are surprised that they actually like talking about something other than football, hunting, and business. One man even said that he couldn't believe that he'd been talking about all "that other stuff" for so long and never talking about the most important things in life. For many of them, a key verse is Proverbs 27:17—"As iron sharpens iron, a friend sharpens a friend."

And amazingly, shining light on these areas of life rather than pretending that everything is just great actually makes things better. To try to ignore these very real areas and tell yourself *I won't lust, I won't lust* is like that old game we'd play on one another, saying, "Don't think about a black stallion running over a snowy field." Instead of telling ourself what not to think about, we need to fill our mind with good things—how to please our spouse, give our children a good memory, or find ways to reach out to others.

Many men are afraid of the label *accountability group* since it conjures up images of telling secrets about oneself, then sobbing uncontrollably in front of the rest of the group. But think of it in terms of a safe place where a bunch of guys can discover they're not alone in their struggles. J. P., an executive for a large Detroit business, hesitated to join his friend from church for breakfast because he wasn't sure he needed "that stuff." But two Scriptures convinced him to at least give it a try: The account of the fellowship of David and Jonathan in 1 Samuel—especially chapter 20 where they confided in each other as Saul's treachery increased—and Ecclesiastes 4:9-10, which says, "Two people can accomplish more than twice as much as one; they get a better return for their labor. If one person falls, the other can reach out and help. But people who are alone when they fall are in real trouble."

Once J. P. decided to give the group a try, he was amazed at how much he enjoyed it. Finally he understood what his wife thought was so great about the women's retreats she'd been attending for the past decade through their church.

That's what's exciting about the growing movement known as Promise Keepers. Founded by former football coach Bill McCartney, the movement not only motivates men to keep their word to Jesus Christ, their wives, children, churches, and communities but also shows them *how* to do that.

Promise Keepers started in Boulder, Colorado, a few years ago with just a few hundred men. Today, Promise Keepers gatherings pack out stadiums all over the United States. And it gives men a familiar setting—a football stadium—where they can do "guy things" such as holler and cheer. In the summer of 1995, I worked at the Focus on the Family book booth at the Denver Promise Keepers gathering. Believe me, it's a thrill to hear fifty thousand men cheer not for opposing football teams but for the things of the Lord, including for being the husbands and fathers he has called them to be.

TRY A LITTLE POLITE HONESTY

When I'm speaking at a couples' conference, the *men* don't come up to me later and say, "Well, she should just know what I need." I think that's because men are more direct in telling others what they want. And women keep having this idea that if we are truly loved, our minds will be read and every little wish we have will be anticipated. That's too heavy a burden to put on another human being. Remember, even God wants us to express our needs and desires to him—and he's the only one who can truly read our minds. How is it that we're willing to present our needs to our heavenly Father even though he already knows them, but we often refuse the same courtesy to our human spouses—who really need us to tell them?

Believe me, ladies, silence is not an effective form of power. All it does is create even more anger—first within yourself and then in your husband as he realizes you're upset but he doesn't have a clue why.

How's this for a typical exchange? The husband comes home from a Saturday morning trip to the hardware store. As he walks into the kitchen, his wife throws him a look that lets him know she's upset with him. Several questions run across his mind. Did he forget to get something she asked him to? Did she have something else planned for today? Did he forget to put the seat down again?

So, being a typical male, he dares to ask, "What's wrong?"

What's her response? I don't even have to tell you, do I? She shoots him a dagger-filled look and says, "Nothing."

So what does he do? He says, "Oh," and starts sorting through the daily mail.

Now she's really upset at him. Why? He asked and she answered. But she lied. Because plenty is wrong, but she—or should I say *we?*—wants him to somehow "just know."

Would it kill her (us!) to say, "I'm upset because you promised to pick up the dry cleaning since the hardware store is right next to the shop. And the dress I wanted to wear to the wedding this afternoon is in that order."

That gives him a chance to slap his forehead and rush out to get it or, if he's really a quick thinker, to wrap her in a hug, say that he's sorry that he forgot, and suggest that she wear the blue dress that shows off her great waistline instead. Either way, you get the point: The problem is going to be solved only if he's allowed into the secret of what he did wrong.

And when we keep quiet about our feelings, why do we blame our husbands for daring to assume that everything is all right? We might have grown up with our mothers anticipating our every need, but we're adults now (supposedly), and we need to communicate directly.

Of course it's difficult to keep working at expressing your needs in a nonthreatening way, but don't give up. Let me end with this wonderful summary that may help you find those ways to keep reaching out to each other: Early in the first chapter of *His Needs, Her Needs,* author Willard F. Harley Jr. gives a quick overview of what the separate genders need: "Her needs tend to be: affection, conversation, honesty and openness, financial support and family commitment. His needs tend to be for sexual fulfillment, recreational companionship, attractive spouse, domestic support, and admiration."[3]

So enjoy the differences! Your communication adventure is in full swing.

SIMPLE REMINDERS

1. Hinting, pouting, and sighing won't get the desired results. You have to ask clearly.
2. Try presenting your case in a simple three-part outline: State the problem, identify the cause, and offer a solution.
3. Families are often spared heartache when the husband isn't required to read his wife's mind.
4. Recognizing the five languages of love—words, gifts, quality time, touch, and acts of service—provides greater insight into our mate.
5. People tend to express love the way they'd like to be loved.
6. An accountability group is just a fancy term for friends getting together and asking each other how things are really going.
7. Many men discover that they actually like talking about something other than football, hunting, and business.

8. Women need women to talk to. (And talk to. And talk to.)
9. Mind reading should not be your expected form of communication.
10. Enjoy the differences between men and women.

DISCUSSION QUESTIONS

1. Have you ever expected your spouse to read your mind? What happened?
2. How can spouses help one another in this area?
3. Have you ever benefitted from an accountability group? If so, how?
4. What advice do you have for young wives who expect their husbands to read their minds?
5. What advice do you have for young husbands in this area?

CHAPTER 6

Adults Are Just Tall Children

HEN Harry S. Truman graduated from high school, he anticipated getting a favored young teacher's traditional kiss. When his turn came, she dismissed him with "You don't deserve a kiss." Years later, when he became president of the United States, he asked one of his aides, a longtime friend and graduate of that same class, if he thought the teacher would give him a kiss *now*.

As a former educator, I'm appalled by that teacher's unprofessionalism, wantonness, and downright disregard for a student's self-esteem. But I tell the oft-repeated story to illustrate how we hold the hurts of our youth close to us even during adulthood.

When I first married, I didn't know that adults are just tall children. I thought that once I'd achieved that physical status, I would automatically know how to do things and would always make the right decisions. I've finally learned that all too often, we adults carry into all our new relationships who we are from our previous experiences.

I love watching the wedding ceremony, with the beautiful bride, the beaming groom, and the confused flower girl and ring bearer. But I always watch for the gesture that symbolizes to me the couple's expectations for their marriage—the lighting of the unity candle. At the appropriate moment in the ceremony, the bride and groom each take a lit candle and join their flames to light a larger candle. I hold my breath then, wondering if the couple will naively blow out their individual candles, thinking they are now merged into one being.

If they do not blow out the individual flames, I am encouraged to think that they are more realistic and understand they are bringing their backgrounds with them into this committed relationship.

One of my friends disagrees with my view of the unity candle, though. She says blowing out the individual candles is a symbol of what the couple is asking God to do with them: "A man leaves his father and mother and is joined to his wife, and the two are united into one" (Genesis 2:24). Rather than symbolizing the extinguishing of their individual personalities, it actually underscores the fact that they are two different people. That's the very reason they need *God* to unite them into one: It's not going to happen otherwise!

I love the story of what actually happened at this friend's wedding: Someone tried to help out by lighting the unity candle before the ceremony, but that only resulted in the wick being burned down to about one-eighth of an inch and buried in wax. The bride and groom spent what seemed like an eternity to them (probably a minute and a half in real time) trying to light the thing, until finally the frustrated groom yanked it off the stand and dug the wick out so they could light it. Then it promptly extinguished itself! What a delightful illustration of the struggle for unity each married couple will face!

Either way, I hope you realized early in your relationship that you and your spouse did not extinguish your individual personalities at the altar.

CHILDHOOD BAGGAGE

Believe me, you bring who you are to your marriage. So understanding your mate's history is vital to understanding the dynamics of your marriage. Let's look at some potential problem areas:

Home and car maintenance

Did his father scoff at his attempts at household repairs? Then he probably won't feel confident about repairing things around the house. Albert has several advanced degrees and is fluent in French and German in addition to English, but to the great frustration of his wife, Roz, he refused to do even the simplest household repairs, preferring, as he said, "to leave such things to the experts."

When they were first married, Roz tried several different ways to get him interested, beginning with gentle nudges—"Honey, the faucet is dripping. While you're out this afternoon, would it be possible to stop by the hardware store? I'd love to have this taken care of before the Taylors come over for dinner." When Albert continued to ignore the drips, Roz found her frustration turning into nagging: "When are you going to fix this faucet? I told you about it two weeks ago, and I'm getting tired of hearing the Chinese Water Torture." From there it was all too easy to attempt to shame him: "I can't believe you have two master's degrees and a doctorate, and could be dropped into the middle of Paris on a moment's notice and sound as though you have lived there all your life, but you still can't remember to take care of a simple drip. Too bad they don't give degrees in forgetfulness; you'd have enough to cover our living-room wall! I can see right now that if I want anything practical done in this marriage, I'll have to do it myself."

Roz went to the hardware store that afternoon and brought home the needed supplies and a handyman book, which she displayed on the kitchen counter. Albert ignored it all, and Roz wound up reading the step-by-step directions as she replaced the faucet washer the next afternoon, grumbling all the while.

The following weekend, the two of them were at Albert's parents' for dinner. During the salad course, Roz discovered that the pepper mill was jammed, so she handed it to Albert, asking for his help. Immediately his father said, "Better pass that over to me. Old

'Fumble Fingers' won't be able to fix it. I've never seen a kid as useless around the house as he was."

Without a word, Albert handed the mill to his father while Roz stared at the bland expression on her husband's face. Suddenly her own cheeks burned with the memory of the harsh things she had said to him over the faucet. It wasn't his lack of interest but his lack of confidence that kept him from taking care of the problem! In that moment, she resolved to affirm him more and lighten up on the expectations. And she would stop demanding that he fit a role he wasn't comfortable with.

Handling responsibility

Was he appointed the man of the house at too early an age? Increasing divorce rates and untimely parental deaths have thrust far too many youngsters into responsibility for which they aren't prepared. Brent had just turned twelve when his father was diagnosed with advanced lung cancer that took his life within two months. The day after the funeral, Brent's mother told him that he was the man of the family now and would need to take on many of his father's responsibilities, including lawn care and car maintenance. Outwardly, Brent nodded solemnly, but inside, panic welled. He knew that his father had handled those chores perfectly; he didn't know that reaching such expertise had been a learning process. And because Brent couldn't do things as well or as quickly as his father, he began to shrink from doing them at all. He began to "forget" to trim the grass around the flower beds; soon he "forgot" to mow the grass. His mother tried scolding him, but when she pointed out a sloppy job, he'd just agree to redo it and then conveniently forget again. Brent carried these same passive/aggressive tendencies over into marriage, exasperating his wife to the point that their marriage was threatened. It finally took professional Christian counseling to address some of those deep-set tendencies.

Starting a family

Was she expected to care for numerous younger siblings? She may not want to start a family for several years. Sally was the oldest of seven children, and by the time she was a high school sophomore, the evening care of the household was turned over to her. Thus, when she came home from school, she would oversee the homework of the others, prepare dinner, wash a load or two of clothes, direct kitchen cleanup, including deciding whose turn it was to wash the dishes, and finally supervise bath time. Only then was she free to turn to her own homework.

Often Sally longed to take part in after-school activities, such as a class play, but she knew her mother depended on her to help with the younger children, especially since the third grader had been labeled a "slow learner" by her teacher and needed extra attention with homework.

The pattern continued even after high school graduation as Sally hurried home from her warehouse job at a greeting card company to prepare dinner and do the wash. When Dane, a coworker, asked her to a movie, she agreed, but added that the 9:30 P.M. movie would fit her schedule better. Accepting a dinner invitation from Dane created a crisis between Sally and her mother, who continued to demand that as the oldest child, Sally had a responsibility to guide the younger ones.

It's no wonder that when Dane asked Sally to marry him, she quickly accepted, "just to get some rest," as she later confessed. They hadn't talked before marriage about when to have their own babies, but when Dane wanted to start a family right away, Sally was appalled and refused to talk about it. It took several months of intense discussion before the truth came out: Sally felt as though she had lost her own youth and needed time for herself. Suddenly Dane understood what his grandmother meant when she once said, "Small families produce large families; large families produce small families."

Budgeting

Did your spouse's parents anticipate every need and make sure money was always available? That was the struggle Wayne and Penny had to work through.

During World War II, Wayne's grandfather propelled his manufacturing business into family wealth. When Wayne left for college, his father handed him a checkbook with instructions to "Study hard, have fun, and call home whenever the balance gets below one hundred dollars." Obviously, Wayne bought whatever he wanted and never had to postpone a purchase or make a choice between any two items. He carried that same attitude over into his marriage to Penny, even though his parents were no longer paying his expenses and his entry-level position into the family business, "to learn the ropes," as his grandfather insisted, did not provide enough to satisfy every want. Penny and Wayne had more than a few long talks at the kitchen table with the checkbook open between them. To have to account for his spending was a form of outside control that Wayne was uncomfortable with. Because of his background, it took a while for Wayne to become financially responsible.

Penny came from an entirely different background. While money meant power and freedom to Wayne, to her it meant security. Her name, in fact, resulted from her having been born at a time when, as her father said, they "didn't have a penny." Her early life was filled with memories of her mother stretching a pot of beans flavored with ham hocks to last three days or of her father walking to his factory job with a cloth sack in his jacket pocket in case he found discarded aluminum cans that he could turn in for a few cents each weekend.

Penny learned to sew early, which provided her not only with a nicer wardrobe but also with a way to earn college money. And once she was settled into her dorm, she quickly discovered a number of wealthy coeds who were willing to pay dearly to have a favorite outfit repaired immediately. Upon graduation, Penny took great comfort not only in having earned her degree but also in entering marriage debt free. She hadn't considered that Wayne's experience of having money run through his fingers would over-shadow her attempts at keeping to a budget that would allow them to buy their own home within two years. Until they each under-stood what money meant to the other, they continued to have heated discussions.

Childhood abuse

Was either of you sexually molested as a child? This area is so complex that I must stress the importance of professional Christian counseling to deal with it. But even though it is difficult to work through, Len and Della are glad they did, especially as they see the difference it's made in their home. In addition to Della's sexual disinterest, it seemed as though she was angry most of the time. And, of course, that anger spilled out toward Len in the form of extreme criticism. Len says that no matter what he did, he couldn't please her.

His response was generally to take her rejection and anger personally or to blame her for not getting over her long-ago trauma. But eventually Len came to understand that his wife's disinterest in a sexual relationship was neither his fault nor hers. Through counseling, they were able to examine and gradually change the situation that had imprisoned them both for a long time.

Insecurity

If someone whose opinion meant a lot told one of you: "You'll never amount to anything," you might unconsciously gather mate-rial goods and drive the newest cars to prove that person wrong. When Max's girlfriend dumped him for the banker's son, she told him that she liked the finer things in life, and she felt that Max would always be a flannel-shirt type of guy who wouldn't know a salad fork from a forklift.

Within a year, Max met and married Heather, who appreciated his sense of humor and hard work. While he finally recovered from the girl who dumped him, he never recovered from her comment. Shortly after Heather and Max married, he insisted upon building their home in an exclusive neighborhood and furnishing it through the town's most expensive interior designer. And he always made sure his old girlfriend's cousin, a former teammate, saw his new car each year.

The intense accumulation of goods undoubtedly would have continued at the same rate if Heather hadn't balked at Max's insistence that they buy season tickets to the opera. Their interests were more in the area of Broadway musicals, so she was bewildered by this action. "Max, who is it that you keep trying to impress?" she finally blurted out one afternoon. "It can't be me, because I love *you*—not all these things."

Only then did Max admit to her—and himself—that the flannel-shirt comment had stirred up his deep insecurity. Once he realized that he had been shouting, "Look how wrong you were!" at someone who was no longer a part of his life, he could slow down and enjoy the results of his hard work—and his loving wife.

Trust

Was either of you abandoned as a child? You may have trouble trusting. Neither of Sophie's parents were available during her childhood—her father traveled a lot, and her mother preferred the country-dancing scene to reading stories to her little daughter. So even though Sophie hadn't been dumped by the side of the road, she had been emotionally abandoned. As she grew up, she decided that she could depend on no one but herself, and she began to move through life with her emotions securely protected behind a thick wall.

This lack of trust is also common within families shattered by numerous dysfunctions, including alcoholism. One woman commented about the emotional wall she and her siblings shared: "To the outside world, we're all high achievers. But it took thirty-seven years for the Lord to bring me to the place where I could say, 'I am a worthwhile person.' But if I had shared my feelings of worthlessness, my friends would have been astounded. They were envying me. Me. The one carrying those great hurts."

Counselors often say that the children of alcoholics typically have three shared characteristics: They don't talk; they don't trust; they don't feel. Jim Broome, cofounder of the Detroit-based Alcoholics for Christ, comments, "For their own sanity, they've had to cover their true feelings. And they're so good at it, they honestly don't realize they've buried all those hurts. They're great with the tough-guy act. But inside they're dying a little more each day, desperately needing direction but not able to trust anyone to help."

Fighting An Invisible Goliath

Lack of self-worth in the child is going to affect his future marriage.

One person who knows just how powerfully childhood baggage can affect a marriage is Christian songwriter and singer David Meece. Over lunch at a Manhattan restaurant, he told me about the childhood baggage he'd brought to his marriage.[1]

"My dad's drinking was a big secret the entire family carried, but nobody talked about it—not even to one another," he said. "I was so bound by 'family loyalty' and so out of touch with my own feelings that only in the last few years have I been able to talk about my dad. If I thought about my childhood at all before that, it was only to say, 'Well, it's over; that was in the past.' It took a long time to admit even to myself that unresolved conflicts were still gnawing at me."

And those unresolved conflicts, of course, carried over to his relationship with his wife, Debbie.

David stressed that his father wasn't a derelict; in fact, he was a pharmacist. He was a classic Dr. Jekyll and Mr. Hyde—gentle when he wasn't drinking or taking drugs, evil when he was. At the drugstore, of course, he had access to anything he wanted, so he'd often come home from work incoherent.

David's dad and mom argued a lot, and the arguments usually ended with his father beating his mother for what he thought were good reasons.

Even in that classy New York restaurant, David's eyes often took on that faraway look as he remembered scenes from his youth. One winter afternoon his parents were on the slippery driveway when his dad threw his mother down and tried to run over her with the car. David wanted to help her—but what do you do when you're in the fifth grade?

"I lived with the thought that somehow I'd caused my dad to drink," he says. "Once when I was about ten, he took us to a high school football game I really wanted to see. He'd been nice about it when I asked him, but by halftime he'd started drinking, and his personality changed within minutes. He argued with my mom and even tried to strangle her on our way back to the car. All the way home he swerved in and out of traffic; I thought we were going to die.

"I sat in the backseat thinking, *It's all my fault this happened. If I hadn't wanted to go to the game, he wouldn't have done that.*"

Amazingly, his mother kept David and his siblings in church—and in the choir. At the time, he didn't see the contrast between the woman encouraging his interest in music and the one trying to protect herself from her husband's fist. "That's just the way things were," he said.

After one particularly violent scene in which the father threatened the children, the mother forced him out of the house. They divorced soon after. "I didn't see him again until my high school graduation six years later," David says. "He just showed up and said, 'Congratulations.' I answered, 'Thanks,' and that was that."

Since David had grown up in the church, he took it for granted that he was a Christian. But in his sophomore year at Peabody, as he questioned whether music was really what he wanted to follow for the rest of his life, he started reading philosophy books. "The more I read, the more I realized I didn't know much about the faith I claimed. Soon I was reading every Christian book I could find," he said.

"One afternoon, alone in my dorm, I kept running into the phrase 'personal relationship with Jesus.' I didn't know what that meant, but I wanted it," he said. "I bowed my head at my desk and said, 'Lord, I really want you as a living spirit in my life.' In those moments, not only did I give myself but my music as well to him."

Shortly after he became a Christian, he met Debbie, a viola major. They married a year after David graduated.

"But I never talked about my father," David said, "so I'm sure she didn't know what she was getting into."

It didn't take long for David's early experiences to affect their marriage. He never became violent, but no one—not even Debbie—could get close to him.

"Everybody thought of me as a nice guy and an amazingly hard worker, who was something of a mystery," he said. "It wasn't as though I was trying to be distant; I just didn't know how to talk about anything of importance. I was king of the emotional walls."

"Poor Debbie watched my stress increase from nervousness to panic attacks and even blackouts," David said. "More than once she found me curled into a fetal position or crying endlessly. We had two beautiful children by then, and at times she must have felt as though she had three of us to care for."

Eventually, after internal and external pressures landed David in the hospital with what appeared to be a heart attack, a perceptive doctor urged him to see a counselor. David refused to go at first, but Debbie went, determined to find some answers. She was so amazed at what she learned about childhood dynamics that she insisted he attend.

It still took David a while to go, but when he finally showed up, the counselor got him talking within minutes because she knew the right questions to ask.

"She'd say, 'You're tough on yourself, aren't you?' or 'You need the approval of others, don't you?' and I'm sitting there thinking, *Yeah! How does she know that?"* David recalled.

Gradually, he started to apply a new perspective to whatever was going on in his life. When he faced a problem, perhaps with a promoter, he'd ask himself, "What's a godly response?"

Soon, the principles he was learning in counseling were opening new emotional doors.

"I realized that the only way to emotional freedom was for me to work through to the place where I could forgive my dad. One night in a hotel room, I paced the floor. Finally I dropped to my knees and said, 'Lord, I genuinely want to *feel* forgiveness.' In those moments, my hurts melted away. Suddenly I could love my dad as he was. I looked past what he had done and saw a hurting man fighting his own inadequacies, making the wrong choice to turn to alcohol to soothe the pain. For the first time I saw his pain instead of mine."

As the emotional healing continued, David began to display openness and compassion for others."If we understand our need for control or approval, we can make changes that will help us keep our friends and our self-respect," David said.

"When we're first struggling with who we are, many of us need to say to another person, 'My dad was an alcoholic.' But some people never get beyond that, of course, wanting people to feel sorry for them. But the real growth comes as we move ahead."

So there you have it, directly from someone who knows that if you're carrying emotional baggage left over from your childhood, it *is* affecting your marriage. But the good news is that you *can* examine the trauma, deal with it, and let it go. Sure, childhood experiences affect marriages, but no one has to be controlled by them.

So, where do you find help? Start by asking the Lord that question. As you pray for his guidance, he will begin to open doors of healing for you—whether through his Word, a counselor, a trusted friend, a support group, or special insight. Yesterday's trauma does not have to control you—or your marriage.

SIMPLE REMINDERS

1. We carry into all our new relationships who we are from our previous experiences.
2. Blowing out the individual wedding candles does not extinguish who we are.
3. Understanding your mate's history will give you insight into his or her present action.
4. The children of alcoholics have three familiar characteristics: They don't talk; they don't trust; they don't feel.
5. The only way to emotional freedom is to work through to the place where you can forgive those who have hurt you.
6. If we understand our need for control or approval, we can make changes that will help us strengthen our marriage.
7. Sure, childhood experiences affect marriages, but no one has to be controlled by them.

DISCUSSION QUESTIONS

1. What childhood baggage did you bring to your marriage?

2. How did it affect your relationship with your spouse?
3. How are you working through that baggage to achieve emotional freedom?
4. Have you needed to forgive someone from your past?
5. How has that process affected your marriage?

CHAPTER 7

Battle the Battle, Not Each Other

R ECENTLY I stopped by a friend's office and noticed a dozen red roses accompanied by a card that said "Happy anniversary to my darling wife." I offered my good wishes and asked how long she'd been married.

Cathy beamed. "Oh, twenty-eight years," she said. Then added, "Fifteen of the best years of my life!"

It seems that for the first thirteen years of marriage, she and her husband just barely stayed together as they battled unfulfilled expectations, misunderstandings, arguments logjammed on unrelated issues, in-law problems—you name it. It wasn't until they made a conscious decision to get serious about working at a good relationship that they turned their marriage around. That's when they transformed a battleground into an emotionally safe harbor.

Don and I had our share of dumb arguments in our marriage, too. But in all that time, I stomped my foot only once to emphasize a point—and put it right into the dog's dish! Not only did that destroy the spirit of the moment (it's difficult to maintain a self-righteous argument with Alpo on your toes), but it also taught us the value of laughter in relieving a tense moment.

That humor came in handy quite often. Once, in a surge of ethnic pride, I designated Tuesday as "German night" (my background) and Thursday as "Scottish night" (Don's background). I'd gleaned several recipes from Don's tiny, highlander grandmother, and I enjoyed making "toad in the hole" and "hot pot" to her specifications.

My German dinners usually featured the sausage, cabbage, and heavily seasoned roasts that I remembered from my own childhood. But Don insisted I was never to serve my favorite: liver and onions. I had no problem with his directive until I found a recipe for *Leber Klosse*—German liver dumplings. I was convinced that if I disguised the liver, Don would discover that he enjoyed it, too.

So after persuading our reluctant butcher to run the heaviest liver through his grinder, I mixed the disgusting-looking result with seasoned flour and produced dumplings that looked only slightly gray when boiled in broth.

After serving a big salad, I set the bowl of hot dumplings on the table. Our Scottish terrier, MacDuff, saw the rising steam and immediately sat up to beg. (Don would occasionally toss him a tidbit, which MacDuff would catch in midair. And that dog would eat anything tossed his way—even bread and cooked carrots.)

Don studied the dumplings for several moments before asking, "What *is* this?"

"*Leber Klosse,*" I chirped, hoping he wouldn't ask for more details. "Try them with the broth. They're great."

MacDuff gave a tiny yelp just then to remind us that he was still sitting up, so against my pleas, Don tossed him a dumpling. MacDuff caught it as usual, but this time, the dog who ate everything held the sampling of my culinary skill in his mouth for a moment, studying it. Finally he spat it out onto the kitchen floor and trotted off to lie down in the corner.

Don looked back at me. "That's it, San. If the dog won't eat it, I'm certainly not going to! Whatever this is, don't ever fix it again."

And he got up to prepare himself a peanut butter and jelly sandwich.

What did I do? I could have cried; I could have snarled about the waste of money; I could have tried to make him feel guilty. But I chose to laugh. And I also determined never to make *Leber Klosse* again.

ARGUE THE ARGUMENT, NOT THE PERSONALITY

As I look back on that silly dinner scene I see that we actually handled the situation correctly: Don reacted to the dish and did not attack my potential to cook future dinners. I, in turn, didn't feel belittled and knew that my cooking skills had not failed. The man just didn't like liver—no matter how it was prepared.

In any disagreement, it's important to calmly state facts about your own feelings or perceptions, such as, "I feel unappreciated when you leave your socks for me to pick up." Sure, that may be melodramatic, but it's certainly less personally damaging than a sharp "You always leave your socks for me to pick up. I'm not your servant, you know!"

If you choose the latter statement, you've just set yourself up for an argument that's going to lead to "Everything's always a crisis with you" or "Yeah? Well, maybe when you stop leaving the cap off the toothpaste, then I'll see about my socks."

In such an exchange, nothing is accomplished except sharp words and hurtful jabs. Hardly the way to correct the problem! And more likely to create even deeper resentment.

So should we *compromise?* Hmmm. I've never really liked that word since it suggests that both sides lose something—and losing makes folks resentful. If you allow resentment to build up in any relationship, sooner or later it's going to explode in inappropriate ways. So I prefer the word *negotiate,* which suggests a mutual agreement to work out a problem and includes talking about both sides of the issue.

I think of Bill, a young father of two who wanted to play basketball on Tuesday and Thursday evenings, leaving his wife, Pat, without help with their toddlers. After she'd been with the children all day, she was tired, too, and looked forward to an evening with him after the little ones went to bed. However, Bill's time with the guys was usually lengthened by pizza and cola. His explanation was simple: He needed that downtime since his job was so stressful.

Oops, wrong thing to say, Bill. Pat retorted that her job was stressful, too. And that he ought to just try taking care of two little kids all day long, seven days a week, without a break. Why, he wouldn't even keep both of them while she went to the grocery store in the evening: He always asked her to take one of them with her.

Quickly, rather than a let's-see-how-we-can-work-this-out discussion, their conversation turned into a feuding atmosphere with both saying, "You don't care about my needs."

It took several more weeks of hurt feelings before they finally arrived at the point of saying, "OK, let's talk."

Bill wasn't about to give up his basketball, so no room for change there. And since this was just the guys getting together to exercise, it wasn't a situation where Pat could accompany him to the gym and sit in the stands and enjoy watching him play. But as they tossed out ideas about how they could solve this, one about getting a baby-sitter struck a nerve. What if they got a sitter those nights to allow Pat to participate in something she enjoyed? She could join an aerobics session at the local YMCA or take a class at the community college or just go to the library to enjoy the quiet. When they solved their argument in that way, it became a win/win situation in which both were happy, and no one felt as though martyrdom was the only option.

Their solution worked. And Pat found that as she had special time to look forward to twice a week, she was less grumpy during those days when she knew Bill wouldn't be home until late. And, remarkably, they began to better enjoy the time when they were together.

But what if they hadn't been able to afford a baby-sitter twice a week? Pat would have been willing to "team sit" with another woman whose husband played those same nights. She also would have considered getting the women together for a "girls' night out" with all chipping in to pay the sitter. The important thing is that one spouse not feel as though he or she always makes the sacrifices.

Of course I wish Bill had chosen the servant/leader role and offered to cut down his basketball for these first few years and help his wife parent their children. If his main concern truly was getting exercise, then it would have been wonderful if he had insisted that they get a sitter one night a week so they could work out together at the gym or go for a long prayer-filled walk as they discussed their week and their dreams for their children. But Bill wasn't open to anything other than what he wanted.

Occasionally I do run into caring husbands who take their role of servant/leader most seriously. One of my friends, Mike Yorkey, gave up golf for a few years and moved his tennis matches to early morning so he would be available for his family. But let's face it—not all families have that type of loving leader.

As an aside, let me mention that exercise is important. If you don't exercise in the midst of your stressful schedules, you will be prone to health problems and perhaps even a heart attack. I stopped playing tennis when Don's cancer appeared. In a sense, I traded my health trying to help him keep his. I'm still dealing with the health problems that resulted from my failure to take care of myself during that time. So do find a way for both of you to exercise. The results are worth the effort.

DON'T EXPECT YOUR SPOUSE TO FOLLOW YOUR PARENTS' WAY

Schedules aren't the only thing couples disagree over. Kati and Ken were arguing, as usual, about who should take out the garbage.

The compromise method wasn't working because each thought the other should automatically handle that responsibility. It wasn't until they were continuing the argument over coffee with an older neighbor that they saw what was really happening.

"Wait a minute, you two," the neighbor said. "When you were growing up, who always took care of the garbage?"

Kati answered, "My dad," just as Ken said, "My mom."

The neighbor grinned. "So you're both assuming that your home will be run by the same habits? Sounds like you two need to do a little more talking. Next thing you know, you'll be expecting each other to visit only *your* family at Christmas and carry through the traditions you had as a child."

As Kati and Ken looked at each other with a you-mean-we've-got-more-work-to-do look, the neighbor chuckled. "Welcome to real life, kids. Anytime you want to talk, I'm here. My hubby and I had to go through the same thing. Everybody does—if they're trying to build a real marriage."

I like the insight popular speaker and writer Carole Mayhall offered on same-gender parent identification: "One day, God brought me up short on the matter of comparison. God said to my heart, 'Carole, you're comparing Jack's weaknesses with your father's strengths. If you *must* compare, compare the whole person!'" Carole said she thought long and hard about that and found, to her surprise, that Jack was gifted at a host of things that her father wasn't."[1]

And that destructive comparison can go the other way, too. Claire had grown up in a home where her father was often absent, preferring the company of his bar buddies to that of his family. There were some weeks that Claire wouldn't see him from Friday afternoon after work until late Sunday evening because he would be in the bar's back room in long poker games.

After Claire had been married a little more than a year, her husband was invited to participate in a bridge game after an office meeting. He called to let her know he'd be late. A furious Claire was waiting when he came through the door, and she let him know that she wouldn't tolerate such activity.

"I know where this stuff leads," she spouted. "You've got a reputation to uphold in our church; you can't get involved like this."

Bewildered, he took in the barrage. What was she talking about? He could have responded in kind, letting her know that he'd go out with the boys anytime he jolly well pleased. But he tried to hear beyond the words.

Finally, as the truth dawned on him, he said gently, "It was just a few guys playing bridge for a couple of hours. No gambling went on, and nobody was drinking or fighting. I'm not your dad, honey."

Startled, she stared at him, understanding at last that she was actually yelling at her dad for his absence and projecting that anger onto her husband.

SHOW KINDNESS, EVEN IN THE ARGUMENT

Claire's background taught her to fight both physically and verbally, so she'd stand toe-to-toe with anybody who thought he was going to out-tough her. But today she understands the truth of Proverbs 18:21, "The tongue can kill or nourish life." So rather than always give in to her temptation to use sharp words, she tries to be upbeat and let things roll off her back. Catch her in an analytical mood, and she'll confess that she doesn't know how to fight fair and will lash out at the person rather than stick to the actual issue. But those of us who know her best, know that the tough-guy image is just a facade that protected her in some bad situations long ago.

I hope those of us who identify with Claire's don't-try-to-out-tough-me attitude are also working toward learning to stick to the issue. I'm blessed with a couple of friends like that, who can point out logically where I was wrong without attacking either my reasoning (or lack thereof) or my person.

Some couples have learned to hold hands even as they're arguing. The simple gesture reminds them that they do love each other and that they are not going to leave the other over this matter. I'm impressed with any couple who can offer such a gesture. That's tough to do when two people are irritated with each other. But it is oh, so important.

As one of my widow friends, Peggy, and I talked about what we wish we could do over in our marriages, she said, "I wish I'd known about the talking spoon." Then she explained that when a husband and wife are in the midst of a disagreement, it helps if they will use a spoon as a reminder to discuss the issue rather than get sidetracked. The person holding the spoon gets to talk, and the other person can't interrupt. Then when the speaker is finished, he or she asks the other, "Now what did you hear me say?" And the other responds by repeating the main points. The spoon holder may say, "Yes, thank you" or "No, that's not it. This is what I actually said." But each person is heard. What usually happens when we're in a heated argument is that we try to figure out the next thing we're going to say instead of really listening to each other.

Peggy says her husband was quick-witted and gave snappy comebacks that pulled her away from the point she wanted to make. She would often end up saying the wrong thing or giving in and agreeing to something she didn't like. If they had used the spoon idea, she would have felt more freedom to be calm and express herself in the way she was comfortable.

Don't Use the "D" Word—Ever

The only time I mentioned divorce was when I said it in a teasing way because Jay and Holly—all of three and four at the time— were being particularly rambunctious one evening when I was especially tired. I straightened out yet another of their battles and then looked at Don. "If we ever get divorced, you're taking the kids," I said.

I expected him to tease me back, but instead he looked at me most seriously and replied, "If you ever leave me, you better believe I'll take the kids. I'll fight for 'em for all I'm worth."

I wasn't expecting seriousness nor that tone from a clown, so all I could do was mumble, "Well, I guess we better never get divorced."

I never said that word again.

DON'T TRY TO FOOL YOURSELF

Now somebody reading this may say, "Arguing is never an issue with us. We never disagree." Never? Are you saying you don't even need to negotiate? Hmmm. That means somebody is always giving in. If that's happening, then resentment is building in one of the partners. And, like steam, when it builds up long enough, something is going to blow.

By its very nature, marriage can't help but include conflict. It's how we handle that conflict that becomes important. No two people with differing backgrounds, opinions, and expectations will agree on everything all the time.

Conflict itself is not bad. It's how we handle it—or don't handle it—that causes the important fallout.

I remember an account of Dr. Robert Sprinkle, a Chicago pastor in the early 1980s, whose communication workshops powerfully made the point that avoidance actually makes the conflict worse. To illustrate the point, he'd have two people stand facing each other with palms out, as though they were about to play patty-cake. The first person would then state his frustration over an imagined conflict, patting the hand of the second person with each dramatized complaint. The second person was to accept the pats to his or her palms and could pat the palms of the first person if he/she wished. Gradually, the imagined anger of the first person would subside, and both participants would glance to the instructor with a look of "OK, what now?"

For the next round, the participants were to repeat the activity with one important change: The second person was to back away each time the first person attempted to pat his or her hands. The most amazing thing would happen: The first person would follow, determined to pat the partner's hand even to the point of getting visibly and authentically angry. Often the second partner's backing away would escalate to the point that the second was being chased around the room by the first. Compare this to marriage: How much better to have both partners face and deal with the issue.

PRACTICAL POINTS

Here are a few tried-and-true principles that will help get you through a disagreement:

Pick your time

"Never argue with a hungry man," my mother used to say. And she's right. Look at Esther in the Old Testament. When she had a problem that she wanted to present to her husband, the king, she invited him to a banquet first (Esther 5:4). Now, some would see this as being manipulative. But it was a smart move to make sure his stomach was filled so she could use that as a bridge to his head.

Follow Esther's example: Don't hit each other with everything all at once. The "seven-minute rule" is a good one to follow. Give each other seven minutes after getting home before presenting the latest crisis. And if you need a long discussion, ask, "I have something I'd like to talk to you about. When would be a good time?"

Now, of course, none of this will work if you have a real crisis. I remember the story of the husband who came home grumpy after a tough day at work. His wife had that worried look on her face, so he said, "I don't want to hear any bad news tonight. I won't listen to anything but good news."

She thought for a moment and then said, "Well, the good news is that we have three beautiful children. And *two* of them did not break an arm today."

Give each other space

If your spouse withdraws, let it go for a time. Of course, we know the command not to let the sun go down while we are still angry (Ephesians 4:26), but there are times when one or the other will need space to sort through feelings.

It may be that you need to sleep on it, too, and talk about it in the morning when you're both fresh and clearheaded. The main thing is to agree that you will talk later and settle your differences. (Hey, the verse doesn't say *which* sun!)

Use company manners with each other

Can you accept the idea that your spouse's anger toward you is actually a compliment? Your spouse feels safe with you. He can vent. You're not going to fire her just because she was impatient with you, which could very well be the case if she was short with her boss. But just because we feel safe with someone does not give us the right to be rude. We wouldn't snap at a coworker for dropping the stapler and startling us, but we'll yell rather quickly if that happens at home. What would home be like if we used a bit more of our company manners?

Don't argue when you're both tired

One of our family jokes developed early in our marriage when Don cut off a building disagreement with "Honey, we are both tired. And when we're both tired, *you* say some of the dumbest things."

Don't resort to dirty tricks

One of my aunts told her daughters, "Never try to out-tough your man. If he won't give in, just cry." I'm appalled! I believe crying is the ultimate·manipulation, and I refuse to use it to get my way.

Oh, to my frustration, I do cry when I'm angry. And I confess that I'm not manipulation free.

Unfortunately, I was raised in a community where women weren't allowed to be straightforward, so they felt they had to resort to manipulation. Case in point: Don and I had been married just a few months when we were shopping together and I discovered a stack of cookbooks on sale. I wanted the Betty Crocker *Cookie Book,* but I knew Don would say no. So I pulled *eight* cookbooks off the stack, turned to my young husband, and said, "Honey, look! These are on sale."

He looked at the stack in my arms and exclaimed, "Eight! You don't need eight cookbooks. You may get *one.*"

I smiled. "OK. Thank you, honey."

I'm happy to report that we both finally outgrew those attitudes.

Be creative

I have a young friend who wants to discuss his marriage with his wife, but she refuses to talk about anything beyond the surface problems. He always feels as though he's walking on eggshells around her.

One day, he poured out his frustration to me, saying, "She won't discuss anything. She clams up. I don't want to live like this for the rest of my life, but I'm committed to her and to our marriage. How do I get her to talk?"

I admit I was amazed since normally it's the wife rather than the husband who is asking me how to get the other to communicate. He'd tried the usual routes of picking the right time, helping with the children, etc., but still no depth. So the only thing I could suggest was to leave a notebook out on the kitchen counter and try communicating through that. He could explain his side of the argument and then add something like, "I really am interested in hearing your side of this." That was just different enough that he decided to try it, even saying that he was going to stop on the way home from work to buy a pretty notebook.

The next time I saw him, he was beaming, saying that the notebook idea was working and that they were actually writing back and forth. Amazingly, he learned that she preferred this type of communication because it gave her a chance to think through her response without having to keep up with his quick—and sometimes sharp—wit. And it forced them both to stay with the main issue in both asking and answering the questions, rather than being drawn into an emotional aside that might lead to a personal attack.

Pick your battles wisely since so few of them really matter
Does it really matter where the sofa goes? Don and I had several dumb arguments during the summer of 1981. When his brain cancer was diagnosed one August morning, doctors ordered tests and conferred with serious looks over charts and CAT-scan reports. It was hours before Don and I were left alone for a few minutes. By then his pain had eased enough that he insisted I go home and rest before bringing Jay and Holly, then eight and seven, to visit him that evening.

I stood by his bed for an awkward moment. Finally I leaned over, careful not to bump the IV needle in his arm, and kissed him. "I love you, Donnie."

He read beyond the words. "I know." Then he made an effort to be the old Don, the clown. "Now aren't you glad you didn't quit teaching last year? Looks like you're gonna need that job."

I stammered. "I don't want you to worry about *me.*"

His face contorted. "Well, I do!"

Immediately my arms were around him, and my face was against his neck as we sobbed together. Guilt mixed with my fears. How silly our arguments had been that summer. And, oh, the selfish things we had said. Now all I could say was, "I'm sorry. Forgive me."

He nodded. "Me, too. Oh, San . . ."

As I pulled out of the hospital parking lot, I thought about our crying together. No matter what was ahead, we had been able to say what we needed to. But, oh, the precious time those dumb summer arguments had wasted.

As I write this, the father of one of my young friends is dying of a brain tumor. With sadness the son reports that he's never seen his parents respond so lovingly to each other. When his mother visits his dad at the hospice, she leans over the bed to put her head on his chest. With great effort, her husband pulls his one good arm up ever so slowly and plops it on her back, and then pats her for a long minute. The son is glad that his parents are finally tender after all those years of griping at one another, but he laments, "Why did it take this to make it happen?"

Let me end on an encouraging note: Remember, conflict shows that growth is trying to emerge. So don't give up on each other. The results are worth the effort.

SIMPLE REMINDERS

1. Argue the argument, not the personality.
2. Rather than compromise, try negotiation, which suggests a mutual agreement to work out a problem.
3. Don't expect your spouse to follow your parents' way of doing things.
4. Even when you're nose to nose, remember the truth of Proverbs 18:21—"The tongue can kill or nourish life."
5. Some couples have found it helpful to hold hands in an argument as a reminder to each other of their commitment to the marriage.

6. Try the "talking spoon" as you're working through an intense discussion.
7. Don't use the "D" word—ever.
8. Conflict itself is not bad; it's how we handle it—or don't handle it—that causes the fallout.
9. Use company manners with your spouse.
10. Pick your battles wisely since so few of them really matter.
11. Be encouraged: Conflict shows that growth is trying to emerge.

DISCUSSION QUESTIONS

1. What communication surprises did you run into early in your marriage?
2. What adjustments did you have to make because of the way your parents handled events during your childhood?
3. What is the "dumbest" thing you've ever argued about?
4. What are some creative ways you could deal (or have dealt) with conflict?
5. What have you learned about handling conflict?

CHAPTER 8

Whaddaya Mean, I'm Overdrawn—*Again?*

C RYSTAL'S father had struggled with a gambling problem at one time and had written a few bad checks, so even after his recovery he refused to have a checking account and paid all the family's bills with money orders. Thus, when Crystal and Vernon married, she had never written a check and didn't have the slightest notion of how to balance the statement that arrived each month.

Vernon, on the other hand, had come from a family where the prevailing attitude had been "it's up to the man to make the money and up to the wife to take care of it." And Vernon's mother had been very good at that, including writing all the checks and balancing the checkbook to the penny every month. Vernon couldn't remember having ever seen his father write a check, so he assumed that was something wives did as part of their household responsibilities. He and Crystal were both in for a shock when it came time to pay their first month's bills, since they both assumed the other would handle that. It took a few trips to the library's financial shelves by Vernon and a tearful trip to the bank by Crystal before they felt confident with their checking account.

We shake our heads at such scenarios, but I've met more than one young couple that has been that naive about its family finances. Too often, they act as though the checking account is the *bank's* responsibility. Don and I had our own share of on-the-job training with finances, so here are some of the things we had to learn the hard way. If you dislike budget chapters as much as I do, go ahead and skip this one. But first, glance at the following five points from a veteran:

Pay God first
Even though the tithe is based on a command from the Old Testament rather than the New Testament, I'm convinced that supporting God's work is one of our privileges as Christians. For years, I've helped three missionary families in addition to giving to our local church. But if you aren't sure about how much you should give or where it should go, talk over your giving with the Lord and ask him what he wants you to do. And if you're convinced that you can't give a full monetary tithe right now, consider tithing your time or talent by teaching a Sunday school class or painting a mural for the church nursery. The important thing is to give back to the Lord a portion of what he has given you.

A caution here though: However we decide to pay our tithe, we should do so out of a spirit of thankfulness rather than expect God to pay us back "ten times over" or "a hundredfold"—as some preachers insist. We can never out-give God, of course, but neither does he *owe* us anything. He has promised to supply our *needs* (Phil. 4:19), not our *wants*.

You don't have to have a new car
As soon as you drive a brand-new car off the lot, it suddenly becomes used, so why not start with a good used car? You'll get more of the gadgets you want and save a bundle of money, too.

Don't spend more than 30 percent of your salary on housing
The expression "house poor" is true. You can have a fabulous house and not afford to decorate or entertain the way you want to. And it's no fun to never be able to go out for dinner and a movie because the house payment is too high.

Live on less than you earn

Those are strong words for today's society because we have so many wonderful temptations just crying for our money. The challenge is not to get more money; the challenge is to use wisely what we have. One thing that helps me is to refuse to pay for adventures with a credit card. Even a little bit of debt can start us on a spiraling descent into financial disaster. Besides, being in debt is one sure way to have less than nothing.

Understand what money means to each partner

The way people view money determines how they want to spend it. While money to me means security, to Don it meant freedom. Understanding differences like that can help spouses keep from reacting passionately to each other's spending habits.

MAKE RULES AND KEEP THEM

Well, if you're still with me, let's get serious about this money stuff. The January 1, 1991, radio program of Christian financial advisor Larry Burkett offered four major resolutions we can readily adapt for our financial juggling:

- Use no credit cards
- Reduce existing debt
- Balance your checkbook each month to the penny
- Determine to conquer your biggest personal financial problem—whether it's overspending or impulse buying.

To that list, I would add only this: Pray about every expense, and allow the Lord either to solve your problem or to show you creative ways to deal with it. When I was growing up, more than once I heard older relatives say, "Honey, if you need anything at all, just let me know—and I'll show you how to get along without it!" That attitude certainly stretches the dollars, but there will be times when you need to present your concern to the Lord and watch him take care of it.

Rusty and Wendy determined early in their marriage that they wouldn't charge Christmas gifts for their large family but would rely on special sales and homemade gifts. One year, though, the budget was especially tight, and for one fleeting moment they were tempted to use the charge cards as the holiday approached. Instead, they chose to remain good stewards of what the Lord had provided, agreeing that if he wanted them to have more, he'd provide it.

Two days later, the town manager called Wendy, saying a local family had decided that as their present to each other, they wanted to provide Christmas for a "young, hard-working couple with several children." The manager added, "You and Rusty fit every one of those requirements. Would you help this family celebrate Christmas by accepting their anonymous gifts?"

Wendy agreed and gave the requested ages and sizes of each family member. On the appointed day, she drove their station wagon to the town manager's office, thanking the Lord for his provision of a gift for each child. But when she arrived, she was stunned to see piles of wrapped presents and boxes of food filling the office. By the time all of the items were stowed in her vehicle, there was just barely enough room for a bewildered and thankful Wendy to fit into the driver's seat.

That experience has since become a family reminder of how the Lord provides, as we allow him to.

SAY NO A LOT

We immediately think of saying no to our children's demands for the latest designer clothes, labels, etc. But we also have to say no to ourselves. After all, do we really need that new gadget, video, or outfit? Retailers readily accept our credit cards because they know we'll spend at least 30 percent more if we whip out the plastic instead of paying by cash.

When we lived in New York, Holly was in that insecure teen stage where she wanted to wear the designer clothes we couldn't afford. So we struck up a deal: I would tell her how much our family budget would allow for, say, a new jacket, and she had to make up the difference with her baby-sitting money. My, once she had to shell out *her* hard-earned dollars, she didn't *need* quite so many designer labels. By the time we moved to Colorado Springs, not only had she matured, but she also managed to get wonderfully caught up in the local habit of shopping at the well-stocked thrift stores. In fact, her favorite overcoat came from the Salvation Army store and cost only $2.95.

FREQUENT RESALE SHOPS

I hope your area has Colorado's appreciation of a good resale bargain, too. While I haven't found a business suit there, my gardening clothes come from those racks. In fact, my favorite flannel shirt cost $1.50 and is similar to one I priced at $32 at a mall shop. Get a friend to go with you so you can encourage each other. And have fun with it. One of my friends shops at thrift stores because she and her husband work for a local ministry group. But instead of being grateful that her smaller size and creative flair with clothes allow her to find incredible bargains, she grudgingly acknowledges another's compliment with an explanation that she bought it at the Salvation Army because she and her husband are in ministry and can't afford to shop anyplace else. Some of her outfits make the rest of us drool, but we're afraid to comment because she's such a grump about them.

If you're not comfortable shopping there for yourself, resale stores are a must for children's clothing needs. Jay and Holly were some of the best-dressed toddlers in the church nursery because I shopped garage sales and thrift stores. My favorite size-two summer outfit for Jay consisted of white shorts and brown-and-white shirt—and cost forty-five cents.

MAKE A LIST

Do you know where your money goes? No? Then it's time for a financial inventory—a fancy name for listing the money you have coming in and the amount going out each year.

Make an actual list of your income sources and amounts, savings, and investments. Then list all of your debts—including the house and car. Then subtract one from the other; that gives you your net worth. Now this sounds like a weighty challenge, but you've already done that if you've ever applied for a home loan. I hope you've kept copies of those loan requests. If so, just haul them out again as the first step in the budget process.

When businesses do this, they call it a "balance sheet," which is just the way they keep track of income and outgo—and make sure that it balances. If you do this, not only will you undoubtedly discover that you're worth more than you think, but at the same time, if you're having serious financial problems, you may readily see where they're coming from.

And while you're making a list, further help your family by listing all the important papers, addresses, and other such goodies and where your family can find them. Are you vested in a pension plan? List that address as well. Also list the insurance policies for car, home, and life. Next, list mortgage holder and number, as well as the account numbers for checking and savings accounts.

BUILD AN EMERGENCY FUND

You must begin to save 10 percent of each paycheck. I remember hearing once that most families are two paychecks away from the street. Since I have a real fear of turning into a New York bag lady,

I watch that emergency fund most carefully. Too many folks haven't been following that standard savings recommendation, but it's not too late to start now. It's like that old saying, "There are two good times to plant an oak tree: twenty years ago or right now." So if you didn't "plant your oak tree" twenty years ago, you can still plant it today.

Tax Time Doesn't Have to Be a Hassle

Jane Bryant Quinn often helps folks get organized for taxes. Since she's a confessed disorganized person, I'm helped by her encouragement that I, too, can handle my taxes.[1]

In getting organized, she says we need to keep the following:

Insurance policies
Life, auto, health, and homeowner's (plus all correspondence relating to them). She also suggests keeping old auto and homeowner's policies for three years—just in case.

Taxes
Receipts for deductible items. (Note: You need actual receipts from charitable organizations. The canceled checks alone won't do it.) At least three years' worth of tax returns and the supporting data (six years' worth is better) and records of nondeductible contributions to an Individual Retirement Account.

Bank accounts
All the information received when accounts were opened, monthly statements, canceled checks, passbooks, and statements about certificates of deposit need to be in your files.

Debts
The mortgage, bank-loan records, contracts for installment purchases, and interest statements belong with your tax records. Keep

credit card receipts only until the bills come and you've checked to see that they're accurate.

Investments
Records of mutual funds, retirement accounts and the information you received when you opened your account, brokerage statements on monthly transactions, buy-and-sell confirmations showing what you paid your stockbroker, transaction receipts for Treasury securities, and mutual-fund statements showing all dividend reinvestment. For tax purposes, you need to know what you paid for an investment, what you sold it for, what dividends you received, and any brokerage commissions you paid. (I don't need that information. I hope you do.)

Social Security
Oh, boy. This is one area that I haven't taken care of. I'm supposed to request and keep periodic statements of contributions.

Warranties
Keep all of these in one file folder rather than in the kitchen junk drawer, so you'll know where everything is if something goes on the blink. I have mine together and periodically weed them out as something breaks. But there's a rule, of course: The item will give out three days after the warranty ends. (Do you think the manufacturers have a timed computer chip in the item?)

Wills
Keep copies of both your wills. You *do* have wills, don't you?

MAKE A WILL
Statistics tell us that between 65 and 80 percent of the population does not have a will. Some think they have plenty of time, some have gotten it into their heads that they're going to live forever, and

still others are afraid they'll create a self-fulfilling prophecy. After all, if you have a will drawn up, you might need it.

I hate to be the one to tell you this, but death is not optional. If the Lord tarries, all of us are going to die. And while we wait for him, we are to take all steps necessary to provide for our families (1 Timothy 5:8).

Don and I had always had a handwritten will and even had it witnessed by friends. But since Don had taught business law for years, he knew the safest documents were the official ones, so within a week after his release from the hospital, he called a lawyer. The appointment took less than an hour, but we made sure the property transfers would be done as effortlessly as possible—and without extensive delays. I'll always be grateful for his loving thoughtfulness.

Perhaps you're thinking, *Well, that's fine for people with property, but I don't own enough to go to all the trouble of doing a will.* Do you own more than the shirt on your back? Do you have a savings account? A checking account? Savings bonds? A gold watch that belonged to your grandfather? If so, you want to have a say in how those things are distributed after your death.

And you can't assume that everything will automatically go to your spouse. Since laws vary from state to state, the worst assumption you can make is that the government will do things the way you had hoped. In many states, without a will proclaiming otherwise, a wife receives only one-third to one-half of her husband's estate—even if her income purchased their property—and the rest will go to the children. She will have to keep detailed accounts of everything she spends on the children and has no say in how they spend their portion of the money once they reach legal age.

No will may mean the living expenses will force her to sell the family home, even if it was purchased with money from an earlier inheritance from her parents. And without a will, any distant relative can come swooping in with a claim against the estate, further tying up the proceedings.

Normal wills usually cost only a couple hundred dollars—but they can save us money and hassle. And many lawyers devote their services in the evenings for those families who truly cannot afford to have wills drawn up. A call to your local social services agency will let you know where that's available.

Part of the procedure requires that you provide your lawyer with a list of assets—naming your mortgage holder, insurance agent, bank account number, checking account number, pension holder, and any investments you or your children have. But that's no problem now that you've drawn that list up after reading the earlier part of this chapter.

Wills should change as circumstances change. In New York, I had guardians for Jay and Holly and had asked my local lawyer to be the executor to handle the details of selling our townhouse. Jay and Holly knew that if anything happened to me, they would be sent back to Michigan to live with their guardians, Carl and Marilyn Amann, and would attend the high school where Carl and I had taught together for so many years.

Then when we moved to Colorado Springs and Jay turned eighteen, we had another family meeting in which I reminded Jay that legally he was in charge. (What a way to make sure he prayed for me a lot when I had to go on business trips!) Then I had another will drawn up with my Colorado Springs lawyer, whom I'd accepted based on the recommendation of new friends. That document gives Jay and Holly the legal rights to make their own decisions concerning whether or not to sell our house, and it includes my personal wishes as to what I hope they will choose to do. The lawyer's job will be to offer recommendations based on their situation at the time.

Now, if you'll excuse me, I need to call my folks to see if they've updated their wills lately. Last I heard I was still named as the guardian for my two younger sisters. The problem is that they are now thirty-four and thirty-one, wonderfully healthy, and both have good jobs. I think an update is in order, don't you?

SHOULD THE WIFE WORK OUTSIDE THE HOME?

One of the biggest battles within the church today is between stay-at-home moms and those who work outside the home. Whenever I'm caught up in this argument, I remember a scene from the made-for-TV movie *Masada.* During one scene the Jewish zealot Eleazar discussed the various Jewish sects and told the Roman general who had them under siege, "If you leave us alone, we will kill each other. But you give us a common enemy."

That's what too many of us have forgotten—that we have a common enemy. And instead of fighting each other within the church, we need to fight him. My purpose here is not to tell you whether or not mothers should work outside the home—that's between you, your spouse, and the Lord. But I will offer this observation: Our children grow up far too quickly, and those years cannot be called back. I've worked outside the home since Jay and Holly were young. At first, as a teacher, I had great hours and vacations that coincided with their schedules. But when I changed careers after their father died, they became latchkey children, a situation full of heartache. So allow me to encourage couples considering having the mother work outside the home to pray a lot, talk a lot, and look closely at the facts, including how much it *costs* to have the wife work.

In fact, an article by a *Detroit Free Press* reporter reprinted in our local paper emphasized that given the high cost of child care, transportation, lunches, dry cleaning, and taxes—not to mention extra dinners out and increased clothing costs—wives earning $30,000 or less may discover that the take-home pay isn't worth the added stress the job poses to the family.[2]

For Lars and Olga that meant first asking the Lord how he wanted them to pay the bills and then thinking creatively. They both wanted Olga to stay home with their three young children, but unexpected roof repairs had eroded their savings. One March evening as they finished praying, Olga opened her eyes and found herself studying the decorated Easter egg her Estonian mother had given her several years before. An oval-shaped window had been carefully cut into the front of the blown-out eggshell to reveal a hand-painted scene of a cross on a distant hill. As a child, Olga had often helped her mother prepare similar eggs for friends in their Detroit neighborhood, so with sudden insight she shared her idea with Lars: She would paint one hundred eggs for the local Easter craft show just three weeks away. Of course, that meant they'd have to eat lots of scrambled eggs for a while, but she was convinced she could make several hundred dollars. Lars enthusiastically agreed and then remembered that one of his Chicago cousins used to paint eggs, too. Perhaps she would have some ideas about how to price them. A quick call to her resulted in suggestions for price, display, and simple packaging. Lars took care of the children each evening so Olga could concentrate on the eggs, but he helped most by sincerely praising her efforts and telling her which scenes he thought would bring the highest prices. When the show ended, Olga had netted an incredible $1,327 and had drawn upon her Estonian background for several crafts for the Memorial Day show.

After the birth of their daughter, Chris and Kandy wanted to start a home business that would combine Kandy's cooking talents and Chris's business sense. They batted around names like "Kandy's Candies" but decided they were too limiting. Finally "The Sweet Business" started in their kitchen and rapidly grew beyond selling fancy desserts to trendy coffee shops to include classes in cake decorating, making French pastries, and candy making. Soon they had to move into a downtown store, but since they were the owners, they could set up the baby's crib in the back office—and set their own hours. Both say they'll never go back to the traditional office.

Many couples, though, don't want to start their own business. In fact, Darlene and Gary say their marriage is strong because they *don't* work together. For them, the need for extra income was taken care of when Darlene took on wallpapering and stenciling jobs on occasional evenings and Saturday mornings.

Some women give piano lessons, do alterations, provide child care, do freelance editing, create newsletters for local businesses, or input material on computer disks—all from their homes. Talk to other couples doing what you want to do, and read everything you can get your hands on that will provide fresh ideas.

A young wife and mother of three, Lindsey O'Connor has written an excellent book to help those who want to rethink this whole issue of both parents working full-time outside the home. Titled *Working at Home,* the book suggests ideas and practical tips for setting up a home-based business, including how the children fit in.[3]

But the important thing is first to ask the Lord how to solve your financial problem and then be open to creative and even nontraditional ways of meeting those bills. In Matthew 6:31-33, the Lord said, "So don't worry about having enough food or drink or clothing. Why be like the pagans who are so deeply concerned about these things? Your heavenly Father already knows all your needs, and he will give you all you need from day to day if you live for him and make the Kingdom of God your primary concern."

While we are looking to his provision, though, we must also remember that he expects us to do our part, too. I like the challenge that we are to "pray as though everything depends upon him, and work as though everything depends upon us." After all, while he gives every bird its food, he doesn't throw the food into the nest. So go forward, confident that he cares about this area of our lives and will provide through the talents and interests that he has given us.

SIMPLE REMINDERS

1. Even though the tithe is based on a command from the Old Testament rather than the New Testament, supporting God's work is one of our privileges.
2. You don't have to have a new car. A good used one offers a better deal.
3. Don't spend more than 30 percent of your salary on housing.
4. Live on less than you earn.
5. Understand what money means to each partner.
6. Pray about every expense, and allow the Lord to show you creative ways to solve your problem.
7. Learn to say no.
8. Taking your family's financial inventory isn't as difficult as it sounds.
9. Make a will.
10. Consider the actual cost of having the wife work outside the home.

DISCUSSION QUESTIONS

1. What did you have to learn about finances early in your marriage?
2. What were your greatest financial challenges in those early years?
3. What are your continuing challenges?
4. What are the financial rules your family lives by?
5. What financial advice do you have for young couples?

CHAPTER 9

How Do I Stop This Runaway Train?

DURING one of my oh-poor-little-ole-me times as I scrambled to keep up with all my responsibilities as wife of the chairman of the deacon board and mother of two toddlers, I visited Mrs. Kennedy, an elderly Scottish friend, in a convalescent home. Sitting with her under a beautiful Michigan maple was the most relaxing activity I'd had in weeks. But as she asked about my schedule, I lamented my endless activities. When my litany was finished, Mrs. Kennedy quietly said in her thick brogue, "Ye have a good man and two bonnie babies, and ye don't even know ye're livin'!"

At the time, I thought her comment rather harsh. But now I better understand what she was trying to say: My schedule was so busy that it kept me from counting my blessings.

All I knew then was that I was on a runaway train racing out of control down a steep incline. But if I had looked down, I would have seen that it was *my* hand on the throttle.

GET A HANDLE IN YOUR SCHEDULE
Do you identify with that intensity, too? Then please remember that—barring a handicapped child or two-year-old twins—most of us *do* have control over our days, and we *can* make changes to slow down our schedules. (And even if you have those extra child-rearing challenges, you can ask for help!)

If you're convinced that you can't slow down, let me ask: What are you running to—or from? Is your busyness from joyful serving or from grim-faced obligation? Deep in your gut, are you feeling so insecure that you must keep busy? Family specialist Dennis Rainey says that for a husband who must schedule every minute, "busyness boosts his self-importance by making him feel needed." And it's not just the men who struggle with that.

Somebody out there just said, "But you don't understand my job responsibilities." Oh, yes I do. I used to have one of those jobs that demanded fourteen-hour days and then made me feel guilty for not putting in more time. *Downsizing* has become a household word. According to employment experts, almost 50 percent of the businesses in America have reduced their number of employees and now expect one employee to do the work of at least 1.3 people for the same pay and with less time off.[1] But the morning I realized that if I dropped dead they'd merely step over my body was the morning I started making plans to join a saner organization. We do have power over our circumstances—either to change the situation or change our response to it.

STRESSED OUT?

Stress and overwork are two of the biggest problems for today's young couples. Of course, we all need challenges to send us into the day with adrenaline pumping, but let's not overdo it. Realistically analyze your schedule. Remember the old adage that at the end of life, no one ever said, "I wish I'd spent more time at the office." With sadness, I can hear Don saying, "I wish I could call back all those times I chose to be away." That was just four months before he died.

So if the end of your life were near, how would you wish you had spent your time? That's an important question. If you truly ponder the ramifications, they will force you to analyze how you are investing your life.

And while you're analyzing your schedule is a perfect time to look at your hopes and dreams for your marriage, too. I know several couples who take mini-retreats not only to slow down but to analyze the state of their marriage—where it is and where they want it to go. Cindy and Chuck check into a resort every August to celebrate their wedding anniversary and to decide where they want their marriage to go during the next year, including what activities they'll be involved in at the church. Their goal is to use their time well without getting caught up in the craziness of overcommitment.

But analysis doesn't have to be that formal. Mark and Nikki go out for dinner at their favorite Chinese restaurant, accompanied by a pad of legal-sized paper, twice a year. Sherry and Bill toss all the family-room pillows on the floor in front of the fireplace every couple of months. Patty and Frank go out for coffee Saturday mornings just to say, "How are we doing?" There's more than one way to handle a marriage and scheduling checkup. The important thing is to find your way to connect.

For Kyle and Sharon that analysis meant they had to sell their large house and scale down their lifestyle. When her mother lamented their giving up the house, Sharon gently reminded her, "Mom, it's just a *house*. Our *home* is wherever we are together."

I'm not suggesting that we all sell our worldly goods and trudge off to the hills of Kentucky (as tempting as that is many days). But I am suggesting that we decide what's truly important to us as a family and take those steps to bring that slower, saner pace that allows us to enjoy each other and give our families more time together and more opportunities to serve others.

Remember, many husbands operate on the premise "if it ain't broke, don't fix it" and may need some gentle reminders that regular maintenance will keep it from becoming broken. Again, we're back to the three *A*'s of a good marriage, which we looked at in chapter 4: acceptance, appreciation, and adoration. If you're taking the time to make sure those are in good working order, you'll be a lot closer to slowing down your own runaway train.

Often that slowing begins with our expression of those things we normally keep to ourselves. What if we took time to say such things as "Something I really appreciate about you is . . ." or "I love spending time with you because . . ." or even "I love you because . . ." And in the midst of all that, let's not forget to add an occasional honest-to-goodness apology.

START NOW

Health experts have finally caught on to the fact that the stresses that leave us feeling exhausted are linked to health problems ranging from poor immune function to high blood pressure and heart disease. Recently I expressed concern for a relative's health, saying that she was under too much stress and should allow us to hire some help for her. She vehemently disagreed, saying that God's will would be done. OK, I believe that God is in charge, but in his sovereignty, he gave us dominion over our bodies. We must take good care of whatever health he has given us—and that begins with limiting the stress we allow into our lives.

What do you truly want out of life? I think of how hard my Kentucky grandmother, Mama, worked. In those days before penicillin, she worried about coughs turning into pneumonia and well water becoming contaminated with typhoid, so she kept her supply of dried herbs close at hand. She sewed her own clothing, her husband's shirts, and all the clothing for her eight children. She provided the family's food through her garden and hen house, putting up hundreds of jars of canned goods that would get them through harsh winters when the house was warmed only by a fireplace and the wood-burning kitchen stove. She scrubbed laundry each week over a washboard and made her own soap from bacon drippings and leftover lard.

And still she had time to visit with friends, help a neighbor in a crisis, construct prize-winning quilts, and make incredible gingerbread. I asked Mama once how she managed to accomplish all that without our "time-saving gadgets."

She smiled and said, "Life was different then. And we didn't have to do all that you young people think you have to do."

Yes, life was different then. As a kid, I remember that Sundays were truly days of rest. The stores, the library, and even the gas stations were closed. That was when families visited friends or went on picnics or took Sunday drives. Basically it was a time to regroup. Today, even I occasionally catch up on my shopping on Sunday after church.

And I've pondered her comment that we "young people" are taking on more than we need to. We're back to my "what are you running to—or from" question. We do have choices.

If you're serious about slowing down your runaway "train," start by making a list of everything you do each day. When I did that, I found that work and sleep take up most of the hours, but the other activities give us a good idea of the type of choices we make each day. (For those of you who must supervise your children's homework, let me assure you that this activity *will* pass.)

Study your schedule

Do you really have to do everything that's on your list? Wanda used to iron her husband's shirts until she discovered that the new cleaners at the corner laundered shirts—and even to her husband's specifications of starch on collar and cuffs only.

And I'm assuming that you're analyzing your TV time, too. Isn't it amazing what a time stealer that can be? We didn't watch much TV since Don taught adult education at night and didn't get home until late. But on those rare evenings when he was home, he liked to relax with a good movie after Jay and Holly were in bed—and he liked having me watch with him. So I learned to save the mending or letter writing for that time, and he'd write checks for the bills or polish all of our shoes.

Make adjustments

What can you cut out? One young mother packed away all of her knickknacks, saying she'd rather play with her children than spend time dusting. Another couple realized that their children were just a year or two away from junior high activities at church, which would mean endless hours back and forth to the next town. So they transferred their membership to a good church just a mile from home to save wear and tear on the car—and their family.

As we analyzed our schedule, Don and I decided that my time after work was better spent with Jay and Holly, so we decided to hire a cleaning lady to come every couple of weeks. Don also liked to say, "Don't use dollar time for a dime job" as he reminded me that it was OK for me, a master-degreed teacher with a good salary, to have help.

I caught on to that concept quickly. In fact, in recent years I've even decided that it is actually *biblical* to have a cleaning lady. Look at the obviously perfect Proverbs 31 woman. (Wouldn't you hate living next door to *her?*)

Too many folks concentrate only on verses 15a and 27-28: "She gets up before dawn to prepare breakfast for her household. . . . She carefully watches all that goes on in her household and does not have to bear the consequences of laziness. Her children stand and bless her. Her husband praises her."

I'd love to hear a sermon about verses 15b-16, though: She "plan[s] the day's work for her servant girls. She goes out to inspect a field and buys it; with her earnings she plants a vineyard."

"Servant girls"? Hey, this woman had hired help! And "with her earnings"? That means she earned her own money and then decided how to spend it—not in a self-centered, "this is mine" type of way, but out of her own ability and determination to help her family. She's one tough cookie! And God has placed his blessing upon such a woman!

MARY AND MARTHA

I've heard poor Martha harangued more than any other New Testament woman, but I'd like to see any church, religious organization, or *home* run without a Martha. Let's look at where her bad reputation began: In Luke 10:38-42, we see that she is trying to get a meal together, and her sister isn't interested in helping:

> As Jesus and the disciples continued on their way to Jerusalem, they came to a village where a woman named Martha welcomed them into her home. Her sister, Mary, sat at the Lord's feet, listening to what he taught. But Martha was worrying over the big dinner she was preparing. She came to Jesus and said, "Lord, doesn't it seem unfair to you that my sister just sits here while I do all the work? Tell her to come and help me."
>
> But the Lord said to her, "My dear Martha, you are so upset over all these details! There is really only one thing worth being concerned about. Mary has discovered it—and I won't take it away from her."

This is where the sermons usually end, with reminders about the importance of sitting at the Lord's feet. But Martha's cooking and serving a meal wasn't the problem; her nervous perfectionism was. In fact, we see Martha serving again in John 12:1-2:

> Six days before the Passover ceremonies began, Jesus arrived in Bethany, the home of Lazarus—the man he had raised

121

from the dead. A dinner was prepared in Jesus' honor. Martha served, and Lazarus sat at the table with him.

Look at verse 2 again—*"Martha served,"* and this time without the reprimand. Had the earlier rebuke from the Lord been enough to make her stop her complaining? Or did it take the miracle of the Lord bringing her brother back to life to change her? All of us who have lived through a traumatic event usually come away from it knowing what is truly important in life. Martha's dear brother has been restored to her. That has to have had a major effect on her life—and her attitude. Perhaps there was a calmness about her now that hadn't been there before, and that new peaceful depth radiated out to others.

We, too, can be like Martha, who, having learned her lesson and taken the Lord's reprimand to heart, now serves with a light heart and with light *hand* upon the throttle of her life.

SIMPLE REMINDERS

1. Many times, our schedules are so busy they keep us from counting our blessings.
2. As you're on your runaway train, remember that it is your hand on the throttle.
3. Stress and overwork are two of the biggest problems for today's young couple.
4. Remember that at the end of life, no one ever says, "I wish I'd spent more time at the office."
5. Add marriage and scheduling checkups to your calendar and together decide how you want to spend your time as a family.
6. With your busy schedules, don't forget the three *A*'s of marriage: acceptance, appreciation, and adoration.

7. The stresses that leave us exhausted have been linked to major health problems.
8. We do have control over our schedules—either to change them or find ways to adjust to them.
9. Martha served the Lord after his reprimand, but with a different *attitude*.
10. Involve the Lord in your schedule. Ask him how to pare down the activities. Then follow his direction.

DISCUSSION QUESTIONS

1. What's adding the greatest stress to your life right now?
2. How are you handling it?
3. How do you react to the question, "What are you running to—or from?"
4. What changes have you made—or are you willing to make—to get a handle on your schedule?
5. Do you ever long for the days when life was simpler? What aspect of those times can you incorporate into your schedule today?

CHAPTER 10

Serving the Lord by Serving Others

O NE of the great benefits of learning to stop chasing futile schedules is finding time to reach out to others. When Don was chairman of the deacon board, we didn't have to look for opportunities to serve the Lord—those opportunities came to us as social service groups, concerned landlords, and even police officers let our church know about families in desperate need. Yes, I'm aware that many of those folks made bad decisions that put them into those desperate straits, but I also know that all too often it's a series of unfortunate experiences that pulls a family down. A lengthy illness, a layoff, a traffic accident—all these unplanned events can hit any of us. And too often, the most innocent of all—the children—are the ones who suffer the most. So we were always ready to help rather than judge.

Thus, the board delivered furniture, blankets, clothing, and, most often, groceries to families in the northern part of Wayne, Michigan—"NorWayne" as it was called. As I shopped for the groceries, I always selected the usual staples—potatoes, chicken, hamburger, roast, canned vegetables—but I also put items in the cart that I would want for my children—bananas, raisins, apples, oranges, and a package of cream-filled cookies. And more than once, Don and I emptied our own refrigerator and pantry when the emergency calls came after the stores had closed in our area. I remember one woman who was sleeping under old coats in an unheated apartment. What a joy to not only help her with utility bills and food—and new blankets—but to connect her with the proper organizations that could help her with job training.

"Jesus Loves Me"

I remember one single mother I visited: She had barely kept up with the rent. Her landlord, bless him, dropped the rent by twenty-five dollars, then called the church late one Friday afternoon to express his concern that the family might not have groceries.

The church secretary immediately called me to ask if I could make the delivery since she knew that Don, a teacher and coach, was working a game that night. Last-minute calls were nothing new, so I accepted, called ahead to let the mother know I'd be bringing groceries by, and asked what time would be good for her. Her mumbled answer of "any time" let me know two things: She probably didn't have enough groceries to prepare dinner, and she was embarrassed to be accepting the food.

So by 4:45 that afternoon, I was balancing two large bags of groceries and knocking on a front door that was badly in need of paint. When the mother opened the door, she wouldn't look at me directly, but the toddler on her hip watched me with big blue eyes. I introduced myself, again named the church that had sent me, and offered to set the bags on the table. Still with her eyes downcast, the mother gestured toward the kitchen.

At that time, single mothers were a mystery to me (I'm glad I didn't know that in less than five years, I would be joining their ranks), and I set the bags on the table, wondering how she and her children were surviving. As I turned around, I saw that a little girl of about five had come into the room. Her blonde hair needed a good brushing. She looked at the overflowing bags with wide eyes. I wanted to get out of there so she could be free to pull the groceries out, but her mother needed to stammer an explanation.

"I used to take the kids to church, but with all the trouble me and my husband—my ex now—was having, I got out of the habit. But Elizabeth here learned some songs." She turned toward the little girl. "Sing 'Jesus Loves Me' for the lady."

But the little girl whispered, "I don't wanna," as her mother glared at her.

Feeling awkward about embarrassing the mother, I quickly said, "Oh, that's all right. She doesn't have to sing."

The woman seemed determined to prove that she was a good mother as she glared at the child. "I said sing for the lady."

And so the little girl fixed her eyes someplace behind me and began to whisper, "Jesus loves me, this I know, for the Bible tells me so," while her mother nodded. When the little girl finished singing, I said my good-byes and "God bless" and hurried out the door as the child dove toward the bags on the table.

I wish I'd hugged the little girl instead of merely thanking her for the song. And I wish I'd hugged the mother, too. But that was back in my intense years, and I just didn't hug folks I didn't know. But I could have—and should have—hugged them in the name of Jesus. Even these many years later I think about that little girl who was forced to sing. Undoubtedly, she's now a mother herself, and I pray that the truth of "Jesus Loves Me" has surrounded her and guided her through life.

JUMP-START YOUR MARRIAGE

Since those days of making weekly grocery runs into NorWayne, I've met several other couples who have experienced the joy of serving together. Angie and Hollis, in fact, insist that their marriage got a jump start as they worked on a conference together.

"We rarely talked about anything beyond the children and bills," Angie says. "Then our pastor broke his arm and asked us to help with the missionary conference. We accepted only because we couldn't think of a good reason not to, but it turned out to be the best thing that could have happened to our marriage right then."

Hollis agrees. "I knew Angie was good at carrying out details, but I'd never really seen her in action outside of Christmas. Working with her on the same project gave me a new appreciation for her—and showed our family that Mom and Dad could get excited about what's going on in the world."

Another couple, Mary and Todd, have worked with the local Habitat for Humanity office for several years. "Serving as a family brought structure to our out-of-control schedules," Todd says. "Besides, it gave us something fresh to think about. It's difficult to constantly want the latest gadgets for your home when you see other families who don't have even the basics."

When I changed careers in my early forties, I joined the editorial staff of *Christian Herald* magazine in Chappaqua, New York, and often enjoyed interviewing Christian couples who worked together to make a difference in the lives of others. We interviewed families who had adopted babies with AIDS, used their vacation time to do short-term missionary work in Haiti, or filled their retirement years with traveling in an RV to remodel camp buildings and churches. We even interviewed a family who fought pornography and succeeded in toughening their state's laws.

Numerous couples have influenced their communities by becoming involved in their public schools through participation in PTA functions, meeting with teachers and principals to express support, and volunteering for class functions. And along the way, they often have opportunities to share their faith.

SHARING CHRIST THROUGH REACHING OUT

One Florida couple, Doug and Billie, brought a young unwed mother, Toni, and her toddler daughter into their home for five months until Toni could afford to move into a place of her own. In the process, their love and care led Toni to commit herself to the Lord. In time, she met and married a godly young man who loved her daughter as his own. When Billie visited Toni after the birth of their son, Toni exclaimed her happiness and thanked Billie and her family for being there for her.

Billie says, "Maybe Toni would have made it without us, but maybe not. And we wouldn't have known the joy of being God's instruments to change a life. I wouldn't trade that joy for anything."[1]

Recently I called Ray Stranske of Denver, whom we had featured, along with his wife, Marilyn, in a 1989 cover story. To my delight, I discovered they are still working to advance the cause of Christ. More than fifteen years ago, they founded Hope Communities with the goal of restoring abandoned apartment buildings and old homes and turning them into clean, safe housing. Numerous lives have been changed because this couple was willing to get involved with those who saw no way out of their desperate situations. But as Marilyn said in that 1989 interview, their calling went beyond restoring buildings: "Part of the Christian's calling is to take on the pain and problems caused by evil in the world," she said. "Buildings and programs will burn up. Our work is loving people and building relationships that allow the Lord to work in all of our lives."[2]

And allowing the Lord to work in our lives often results in some of the most interesting miracles.

Jan and Boyd Keefer, a couple from New Mexico, used their grief over the death of their nineteen-year-old son to start a Bible study in their home when one of their son's friends asked questions. And in the midst of their giving to others, the Lord encouraged and blessed their efforts.

As the study grew, attendance often reached twenty or more each week, so the Keefers added a simple supper to allow for even greater fellowship. One particular afternoon, Jan decided to prepare twenty-seven baked potatoes, thinking twenty-five people might attend that night. Instead, thirty-one people showed up. Jan and her husband quietly agreed not to take potatoes, planning to eat later. Jan watched the pile of potatoes diminish, thinking of what she could prepare for the last four people who wouldn't get a potato. But when the line was finished, everyone had a potato and there were still two left in the dish—one each for her and her husband.[3]

Now some folks would say that she had made a mistake, that God wouldn't do a repeat of the "loaves and fishes" miracle with potatoes wrapped in foil. But Jan knows better. After all, she had counted the potatoes *twice*.

So think about it. Does your family need a "jump start"? Begin by finding ways to reach out to others.

A GLASS OF WATER

Often we don't want to get involved with people's needs because we are afraid we can't handle the job or don't have the skills or whatever. But remember that old saying: "God isn't so interested in our *ability* as he is in our *availability.*"

I understand the fears that can keep us from a blessing. In fact, it took me a while to learn the importance of being who I am, and I learned it because of a friendship with Marta Gabre-Tsadick, the first female senator of Ethiopia.

I first met Marta at our Michigan Bible conference. Her very stance announced authority and grace. Stately and beautiful, she was everything I wasn't.

Our pastor, Dr. Bartlett Hess, was at the conference that week, too, and knew Marta's reputation as both a political and spiritual leader. He invited her to speak at our church about the Marxist takeover that had destroyed her beloved Ethiopia—the world's oldest Christian nation.

The date was two months away. Impulsively, I asked Marta to stay with my family the weekend she would speak. Don and I often hosted special speakers, so when Marta graciously accepted, I assumed the matter was settled.

Several weeks later, however, a friend who had visited Marta's home commented that Marta had served her a glass of water from a tray. Outwardly I nodded at how much that sounded like the gracious Marta, but inwardly I cringed.

Serving a glass of water from a tray? I couldn't remember if I even owned a tray, let alone knew how to serve from it. At our home, if someone comes into the kitchen and asks for a drink of water, I'm apt to continue whatever I'm doing and wave toward the cabinets: "Sure. The glasses are up there. The water's in the refrigerator. Help yourself."

So what in the world was I thinking of when I decided to invite someone like *Marta* into our home? As the days passed, I became more tense. I considered buying a tray and practicing with it. However, the thought of stumbling and dumping the water into her lap changed my mind.

My self-imposed misery continued. I even thought of writing to Marta and saying a crisis had forced us to withdraw our offer and that we'd provide a nice motel room instead. Hey! That wasn't a lie. I wasn't sleeping! And anytime I'm not sleeping, I've got a crisis.

Finally, I did what I should have done when the trauma first started—I prayed. I knelt by the old red chair in the study and poured out my insecurities: "Lord, this woman was a prodigy of His Imperial Majesty Halle Salasse, and she says his name as casually as I say an uncle's name. And she's graceful, Lord. She doesn't *walk* into a room, she *glides* into it. What on earth am I doing with her in my home?"

As I prayed, I realized that God already understood my problem, but I needed to hear myself being honest. Then I had the good sense

131

to shut up and listen. Even though I heard no words, a deep calm settled over me. Then it was as though the Lord were saying to my weary spirit, "Marta is doing a good job at being who she is. Why don't you try equally well to be who you are?"

I peeked around at that. With such a revelation, surely a six-foot-twelve-inch angel stood nearby. But no heavenly being was smiling at me, and no shimmering light filled the room. It was still my cluttered study, and the chair was still faded red and threadbare. But *I* was different as this new freedom rushed in. We'd had guests before—I'd just haul out my best company recipes and invite our pastor and wife over, too.

The next week, Don commented on my calmness but didn't ask for a reason. I'm not sure I could have explained it, anyway. I just knew I was at peace.

When the appointed weekend arrived, Marta, her husband, Deme, and their two sons proved to be such delightful guests that I found myself concentrating on the exciting story of their miraculous escape from Ethiopia rather than on myself.

Afterward, Marta offered to help with the dishes, but I insisted she rest before she spoke that evening. Reluctantly, she left the kitchen as I cleared the counter. But in a few minutes she was back. "May I please have a glass of water?" she asked in her softly accented voice.

Right in the middle of wiping the counter, I answered without thinking, "Sure. The glasses are in that cabinet, and the water's in the refrigerator. Help yourself."

Then I turned around and bit the dishcloth as embarrassment swept over me! In my heart I grumbled at the Lord, *Now I know you told me to be myself, but that's carrying this thing a little too far. How could I have spoken like that to Marta, of all people?*

He didn't answer, but I was so busy haranguing him that I couldn't have heard anyway.

That night, as we prepared to leave for the church, Marta gave me a special hug. Then, with her hand on the doorknob, she suddenly turned back to me. Tears were in her eyes.

"Thank you for opening your home to us this weekend. For two years we have not felt part of a family until now," she said. "We had to leave our families behind—our brothers and our parents. And at our last good-bye, we could not hold the hug for a long moment because we knew their future safety would be in that surprised 'But we didn't know they were leaving!' when the soldiers would question them about our whereabouts. How we have missed them. . . ." She paused, remembering. Then she said, "Thank you for allowing us to be part of *your* family. Thank you for opening your home this weekend. Thank you for letting me get my own water."

By then, I was crying, too, and I hugged her while both of our husbands stood awkwardly by. In the months that followed, Marta became a dear sister, a relationship that I would have missed had I continued to allow my insecurities to rob me of the joy—and even the *fun*—of being who I truly am.[4]

So ask the Lord to show you, first, who you are in him and then how you and your spouse can serve him by serving others. Be open to unusual tasks, but also be confident even as you work together on simple projects that you are about to grow as a couple. Not only will you use your own previously untapped abilities to be the hands of God in this pitiful world but you will also have the opportunity to see your spouse in a different light. So what are you waiting for? Go help someone!

SIMPLE REMINDERS

1. Let's be ready to help rather than judge. A lengthy illness, a layoff, a traffic accident—any of these unplanned events can hit us.

2. Too often, the most innocent of all—the children—are the ones who suffer the most.

3. Many couples have experienced the joy of serving together and have learned to appreciate each other more during the process.

4. It's difficult to want the latest gadgets for your home when you see other families who don't have even the basics.

5. Start with your own interest and find ways to serve the Lord out of that, whether it's caring for neglected children, doing short-term missionary work, or joining with friends to remodel camp buildings and churches.

6. Your influence doesn't have to be dramatic. Numerous couples have influenced their communities by becoming involved in their public schools.

7. "Part of the Christian's calling is to take on the pain and problems caused by evil in the world."

8. Allowing the Lord to work in our lives often results in some of the most interesting miracles.

9. Reaching out to others often provides a needed "jump start" for your family.

10. Remember the old saying: "God isn't so interested in our *ability* as he is in our *availability.*"

DISCUSSION QUESTIONS

1. What experiences in serving the Lord by serving others have you shared with your spouse?

2. What serving experiences have you shared (or would you like to share) with your children?

3. What were the results of some of those experiences? Any miracles?

4. What joys or major lessons have you gained as you have served others?
5. What advice do you have for those looking for ways to show God's love to others?

CHAPTER 11

In-Laws or Outlaws?

One noon hour Donna, a fellow teacher, was particularly upset. Her mother-in-law had called the night before, talked to her son for a few minutes and then said, "Why doesn't Donna ever write?"

So the son had asked Donna the same question after the call. She shrugged and said, "Oh, so *now* your mother wants to be buddies, huh?"

It seems that three years earlier, when Donna and her husband had been dating, his mother had told him that Donna wasn't right for him and that if he went ahead and married her, he would regret it. In a fit of aggravation, he had told Donna what his mother had said. Oops. Well, the marriage went through, but Donna determined never to have anything to do with "that woman."

And that unresolved issue stood between them. Apparently, in a change of heart the mother-in-law had decided to make the best of the situation and accept Donna, but she had never told Donna. What needed to happen was an old-fashioned apology and an invitation to start over. But knowing Donna, she was so much into the power play that I doubt if she would have been willing to give in. And that made everyone lose.

WELCOME TO REALITY

If you have never had problems with your in-laws, skip this chapter. But too often I hear sad stories of relationships that need a fresh touch. Most of the young couples I run into didn't realize they were marrying the entire family as well as the individual when they took their vows. That was a tough lesson for me to learn. My proper—and affluent—northern in-laws were horrified that their son married someone from the hills of Kentucky, and they were quick to remind me of that background. (Fiddlesticks! I was the best thing that ever happened to that family!)

One of their favorite topics of conversation expressed concern about all the "hillbillies" moving into their area. Once, on our way to visit an uncle with Don's parents, we stopped for gasoline next to a family in a dirty car. Don's mother frowned and said, "Well, would you just look at those hillbillies."

At the time, my tactics weren't very effective: I'd usually just offer one of my stern teacher looks and change the subject. After all, a Kentucky saying summed up my challenge: "A person convinced against his will is of the same opinion still."

Over the years, the sniping slowed. I'd like to think that it was my refusal to get into an argument or my consistent dinner invitations (I notice they didn't have any trouble eating "that type" of food.) But in reality, I simply developed more self-respect and they backed down.

It did take a while to get to that point. I remember one Sunday afternoon early in our marriage when Don's mother asked, "Well, what little wifey things did you do this week?"

Just a few days before, I had made chocolate chip cookies with lots of pecans. Don had devoured them, saying, "These are my favorites!"

Wanting to show her that I was taking good care of her son, I chirped, "I made his favorite cookies."

She smiled. "Oh, peanut butter."

I shook my head. "No. Chocolate chip."

She sat straighter. "I've made cookies for him all his life. His favorite kind is *peanut butter!*"

I had the good sense to shut my mouth right then, but you better believe Don heard about that little scene later! Then I asked, "Why did you tell me chocolate chip is your favorite cookie?"

In his typical peacemaking way, he chuckled and said, "Well, chocolate chip is my favorite cookie that *you* make, and peanut butter is my favorite of the ones my *mom* makes."

Even in the short time I'd been married, I'd learned that I wasn't going to change Don and get him to come around to my way of thinking. So I made two decisions: One, never to mention cookies in front of his mother again. And two, not to expect the worst each time we visited her. After all, if we expect the worst, we're going to get it.

That was a rather remarkable conclusion for me to reach. After all, I know how to fight; I'm from Harlan County, Kentucky. When I was speaking in Charleston, South Carolina, last spring, my host asked his friend, who is also from Kentucky, if he knew anything about my birthplace. His friend nodded. "Oh, yeah. I've never met your speaker, but I can tell you this: If she's from Harlan County, she's a scrapper!"

And I am. (Boy, can you imagine what I'd be like without the Lord?!) I try not to take undue pride in my feistiness, but I know how to stand my ground. In fact, when I was a high school teacher in the Detroit area, the only time I raised my voice was when I needed to break up a fight. I'd yell my name: "Break it up; it's Aldrich!"And the students would break it up! I'd grab the two offenders by the arms and march them down to the office. The other students would say, "Boy, you don't want to mess with her. Did you see how she grabbed those guys?"

But that toughness doesn't help one bit when it comes to building a relationship. And that's something Don taught me by his example as he dealt with my folks.

Sure, Don's parents said some rude things, but I have to confess that my own parents weren't thrilled about welcoming the grinning Scotsman who showed up to "steal" their daughter.

In fact, one afternoon the summer before we were married, my parents were particularly standoffish, and I later asked Don, "How could you be so nice to someone who's trying to ignore you?"

He just grinned and said, "San, I'm going to love them now because they're your parents. One of these days I'll love them for themselves—just as they'll love me. In the meantime, we're going to get along."

By the time we'd been married even a short time, Don's sense of humor and determination to be interested in whatever interested my parents moved him solidly into their hearts. In fact, after Don's cancer was diagnosed, and we talked about the possibility that he might die, he said he wanted to be buried in *my* family's plot. "Your mother helped fill the void my mom's death left," he told me, "and she's going to have a rough time when all this is over. Just don't let her spend a lot of time at the cemetery. I won't be there, anyway; I'll be with the Lord."

To this day, they still miss him—just as I do.

ANOTHER ANGLE

It's amazing what a different perspective can offer when it comes to in-laws. Mama Farley loved telling about the mother who was asked about her son's new wife: "Oh, she's so lazy. She expects my son to help her with the dishes and to baby-sit and go grocery shopping with her. I just don't know how long he can keep that pace up."

The visitor shook her head. "Oh, I'm sorry to hear that. How's your daughter's marriage going?"

The mother smiled. "Oh, she has the most wonderful husband! He helps her with the dishes, and he's happy to baby-sit and go grocery shopping with her. He is just wonderful. She's fortunate to have gotten such a good man."

Here are a few solid reminders to help you build the relationship you want with your in-laws:

Refuse to argue
Here's where we have to look to the Lord as our example. Remember, he won people—not arguments.

Again, Don provided a godly example for me as he refused to get upset when one of my relatives would tell him how he *ought* to do something. Don wouldn't argue; he'd just smile and say something such as "Hey, thanks! I appreciate your interest" or "I'll think about that. Thanks." Of course, I teased him that he went ahead and did what he wanted anyway, but he'd remind me that it takes *two* people to have an argument.

One of his major roles within both families was to be the peacemaker. And if he couldn't win over the opposing parties with logic, he'd try emotion: "Hey, life's too short to argue," he'd say. "Let's figure out a way to solve this." (His comment that "life's too short" certainly proved to be prophetic.)

His peacemaking skills have been greatly missed. In fact, the last Aldrich dinner I hosted before Jay, Holly, and I moved to New York was a stark reminder of the void he had left as two of the relatives got into a shouting match and wound up leaving early. I wasn't much help. All I could do was cry as I asked each of them not to go. If Don had been there, the argument wouldn't have progressed to that point. Never had he allowed anyone to leave our home angry.

Keep praying
What if every day we included the Lord in our relationships with our in-laws? What if we began the morning by saying, "Lord, this day is yours. I am yours. Help me act like it."

The Lord already knows we're upset over some of the statements folks make, so we might as well talk to him about them. Remember 1 Samuel 17 when David faced Goliath? In verse 47 he said, "It is [the Lord's] battle, not ours." But often we forget that and try to make every battle our own.

Guard your mouth
Remember, you never have to ask forgiveness for those sharp things you *don't* say.

Consider 1 Kings 19. Elijah was depressed. He'd just come out of a major spiritual victory but was mentally exhausted and physically tired and hungry, so he overreacted and thought he was the only one still fighting the Lord's battles. Look at how he was ministered to—the angel gave him healthy food and water and ordered him to sleep. Only then was he ready to hear instructions about the next step.

Schedule time with your in-laws
Don and I lived halfway between both sets of parents, so it was rare that any of them showed up unexpectedly. But we'd already decided that we needed to keep in touch on a regular basis so they wouldn't be demanding. (Neither one of us did well with the "you never call; you never write" routine.) And it worked! Since they knew we'd either be at their house every other Sunday or have them to ours, they didn't pressure us. If your in-laws live in the same city, you may have to set some loving boundaries early.

Don't go looking for trouble
Remember, if you expect the worst, you'll get the worst. Let some things roll off your back. When Marlene and Kirk were moving into a larger apartment, her father supposedly came to help. Instead he scolded her in front of the movers because the bed frame was dusty. Marlene stammered an excuse about letting it go during the moving process but said that she had planned to polish all the furniture when it was set up in their new home.

Meanwhile, her husband was furious that the father was scolding a grown daughter. But what could have been a bad situation was turned into merely an irritation because they dared to be strong enough to shrug it off. It was a one-time occurrence. But if this had been the father's habit, it would have been appropriate for Kirk to quietly take him aside and remind him that Marlene was a grown woman and that her actions were no longer a reflection on him.

Remember, Jesus has promised us his power, his peace, his purpose, his presence—and trouble. But even as he promises us trouble, he promises to be with us: "Here on earth you will have many trials and sorrows. But take heart, because I have overcome the world" (John 16:33).

Release your mate from having to choose between his mother and his wife

One of my cousins turned every visit with her in-laws into a crisis. All the way home, she'd analyze aloud every word and every look her in-laws had given her that day, much to the exhaustion of her husband. He always felt she was putting him in the middle of a nonexistent argument—hardly the basis for tender feelings. Women especially need to be careful about this one.

Get a proper perspective

Our view of any situation will color the way we see it. I remember a *Reader's Digest* account from years ago of a tourist in a southern state who was driving in the country when he saw a man sitting in a wooden, straight-back chair, from which he would bend over to pull weeds. The driver chuckled, shaking his head, convinced that the stereotypical image of the lazy southerner was true. He turned the corner then and glanced back to laugh again at the gardener. Only from that angle did he notice the crutches propped against the chair. The man wasn't lazy after all but a determined survivor. What a difference a new angle gives us.

What if we looked at the situation from the in-law's view? Pamela said that the day her little boy developed a crush on his first-grade teacher she understood how her mother-in-law must feel that some other woman replaced her in her son's heart. That new perspective strengthened the relationship between the two women.

Find those things you can sincerely praise

Remember that criticism destroys while encouragement builds. Phyllis decided to handle her critical mother-in-law's visits with grace, so she set out each time to find at least two things she could sincerely compliment. One morning, she gave the older woman an impromptu hug and said, "You've raised an incredible son. Thanks!" To her amazement, the verbal sniping slowed down after that.

Be honest with yourself

In family situations, there's what counselors call the *presenting* problem and then the *real* problem. The presenting problem is what appears to be the barrier, while the real problem is something more foundational.

I remember a letter to one of the advice columnists from a mother-in-law. She said, "My daughter-in-law takes good care of my son and my grandchildren, but I can't stand it that she doesn't rinse the soap out of the dishcloth and hang it up to dry. She just throws it into a corner of the sink and leaves it. How can I get her to stop this?"

I like the columnist's answer: "The one thing she does wrong is leave the dishcloth in the sink? What's your *real* beef?"

If you're always complaining about some relatively unimportant but irritating habit of your in-laws, ask yourself what the real problem is.

Offer an unexpected gift

Take this advice and run with it! On Don's thirtieth birthday, I sent his mother thirty sweetheart roses with a little note that said, "I'm so glad you had a baby boy thirty years ago today."

After that, she always introduced me as "my daughter-in-law, the one who sent me the roses."

Every one of her friends had already heard about my creative gift!

Honor your in-laws

Exodus 20:12 says, "Honor your father and mother. Then you will live a long, full life in the land the Lord your God will give you."

Honoring does not mean letting them order you around, pry into your personal finances, tell your kids to get haircuts, or rearrange your cabinets each time they visit. It means honoring their position. Once the child becomes an adult, it's important that a new relationship be built—more "friend to friend" than "parent to child."

Our goal is mutual respect and friendship.

Remember that you are the parent

After Karen became a widow, her father-in-law complained about her keeping the two children in a Christian school and, as he said, "shielding them from the real world."

It crossed her mind to tell him to back off, but instead, like Hannah in 1 Samuel 1:15—when the priest Eli accused her of being drunk—she quietly answered the charges.

"I know you're concerned as a loving grandfather," she said. "But I'm the one who must stand before God and give an account of how my children have been raised. For now I'm convinced that it's best they remain where they are."

Visit other relatives together

I really give Don credit here. One Thanksgiving, he agreed to take a trip to visit my relatives in Kentucky but insisted that we take my parents with us. What a fun time that proved to be. My dad rode shotgun and told stories all along the route. Near Corbin, Kentucky, he pointed out the spot where, as a twenty-three-year-old army sergeant, he'd been hitchhiking home in late 1944. He'd been let off from one ride and meandered toward a shady tree to wait for the next car to take him closer to Harlan where my mother was living with her parents, my beloved Papa and Mama Farley.

As he approached the tree, he saw that a sailor was already waiting. That pleased Dad; he would have someone to talk to until they got rides. Of course, since the other man had been under the tree first, the unspoken code was that he would accept the first ride.

But as my dad got closer to the sailor, he recognized his own brother-in-law, Hurlen Farley, who was on leave, too! Dad gave a whoop of recognition and ran to clasp Uncle Hurlen's hand. They thumped each other on the back and marveled at the chances of meeting like that.Uncle Hurlen would not accept a ride without my dad, and they went on into Harlan together to provide a double surprise for the family.

Story after story rolled out as Dad pointed out landmarks. And I would have missed all that family history if Don hadn't included my parents in our family vacation.

Keep the family ties strong

After Don died, his dad—who had remarried within six months after his first wife died—wasn't sure what to do with me. The first time he had to call, the man I had called *Dad* for more than sixteen years identified himself as Bill. I wasn't about to get tossed aside that quickly, so I quickly responded, "Dad! How good of you to call."

He still had other struggles, though. Because of his own harsh upbringing, he had trouble verbally expressing love for those around him, even his own sons and grandchildren. I remember when the kiddos and I were back from New York for a visit. Before we left, I suggested we hold hands and pray. After my *amen,* I hugged Don's dad and said, "I love you, Dad. I truly do." He didn't answer.

Then Jay and Holly hugged him, both saying, "I love you, Grandpa." But they received only silence, too. I was stunned. But

I let the silence roll on, and we three got into our car and headed home to New York. I made sure that Jay and Holly understood that their grandpa's lack of response wasn't their fault but something in his own background that kept him from saying the words. Then with a feisty set of my jaw, I took on the challenge, determined not only to do the right thing but to have fun seeing how soon I could get those words out of him.

I called him every Saturday to give him a quick report of our life in New York and to have him talk to the kids. Gradually, I got more than silence out of him as I'd sign off with my quick "I love you, Dad." Sometimes I'd hear "That's nice" and once—miracle of miracles—he even muttered, "Me, too" as he hung up. I sat there grinning long after the line was dead!

But the real gift came when we called him on Christmas Eve, 1988. I signed off with my usual, "I love you" and to my great surprise, he answered, "I love you, too" as he hung up. Jay and Holly raced to me from their extensions in the bedroom and basement. "Mom! He said it! He finally said it!" And the three of us celebrated with a big family hug.

THE BEST EXAMPLE

Mother-in-law jokes often present the difficult relationship between a mother-in-law and her son-in-law. But family experts report that in reality the most difficult relationship is the one between the mother-in-law and her daughter-in-law.

The book of Ruth presents the most incredible relationship between two women who were thrust together this way. Both were widowed, and the mother-in-law, Naomi, decided that she would return to her own hometown of Bethlehem in Judah.

Her two widowed daughters-in-law set out with her, but when they got to the border, Naomi tried to send them back, saying she had nothing to offer them. Orpah turned back, but Ruth stayed, saying the words that would become a popular declaration in wedding ceremonies during the 1970s: "I will go wherever you go and live wherever you live. Your people will be my people, and your God will be my God. I will die where you die and will be buried there. May the Lord punish me severely if I allow anything but death to separate us!" (Ruth 1:16-17).

Think about that! Those loving words were spoken from a daughter-in-law to her mother-in-law! And you remember the incredible story of how Naomi taught Ruth the customs of her new culture and, in fact, encouraged her courtship with one of Naomi's distant relatives. Because of that good relationship, both women benefited—Naomi regained her family land, enjoyed security and the love of a precious grandson born to the new marriage, and Ruth gained a place in our Lord's lineage.

Most of us can take a lesson from that account, especially when we're tempted to give in to the frustration of working on a relationship with difficult folks. (Of course, *we're* never difficult ourselves, are we?) One final comment—remember the old saying that reminds us to guard our tongues: "You catch more flies with honey than you do with vinegar."

SIMPLE REMINDERS

1. When you wed, you marry the family as well as the individual.
2. When it comes to in-laws, if you expect the worst, you'll get the worst.
3. Try a new perspective as you consider your in-laws.
4. Invite the Lord into the situation with your in-laws.
5. Guard what you say. You don't have to ask forgiveness for biting your tongue.

6. Release your mate from having to choose between his mother and his wife.
7. Spend time with your in-laws. They'll be less apt to pull at you if they know they have regularly scheduled time with you.
8. Find those things you can sincerely praise.
9. Give unexpected gifts.
10. Remember, you catch more flies with honey than you do with vinegar.

DISCUSSION QUESTIONS

1. Did you have any surprises waiting in the in-law wing when you married?
2. What has provided the greatest blessing in your relationship with your in-laws?
3. What were (or are) your greatest in-law challenges?
4. How did you work (or how are you working) through those challenges?
5. What advice would you have for other couples trying to balance honor of parents with personal autonomy?

CHAPTER 12

Every Circus Needs a Ringmaster

Brian, a young husband, recently sold his one-third share in a multimedia business. The business had a good reputation in town and had appeared successful, so I was surprised by the sale. Since I've known Brian since his childhood, I dared to ask what had prompted his decision.

Brian shrugged. "Equal partnership sounds good in theory, but in practice somebody has to run the show. Every circus needs a ringmaster."

His simple statement made me think of the struggle I see too often in marriage. Joint leadership sounds good in theory, but in practice somebody has to take responsibility.

A HOT TOPIC

This chapter caused arguments among my friends even before I finished it. Last fall, after speaking in Dallas, I was driving to the airport with friends. As we passed the Dallas football stadium, where the Promise Keepers event had just been held, I said, "Someday I want five minutes on the Promise Keepers platform to tell sixty-five thousand men that even a feisty woman like me will submit to a man who's praying and earnestly seeking the Lord's will."

One of my friends jumped on that comment, saying that submission is a nonissue in today's world.

"But I believe God's principles are for our own good," I insisted. "And if he decided that women are to submit to their husbands, then so be it. Submission is not a servant's duty but a protecting umbrella. But I will say that too much emphasis has been put on the woman's part and not enough on the man's responsibility to love with the love of Christ."

Then she snapped that if both partners are praying, there won't be a problem.

I wondered why she was getting so upset, but I didn't want to ask. "Well, that sounds good in theory," I said. "But in reality, marriage often has moments when even godly couples aren't going to agree. When push comes to shove, somebody has to give in. If couples can take turns making decisions, fine. But what about those times when you can't agree?"

Oh, boy. Then she accused me of having an *attitude*. I couldn't believe it. I'm used to having my attitude tossed back at me because I *won't* submit to every man who strolls through my office—but not for upholding the Word. Finally, for the sake of our friendship (and my ride to the airport), we changed the subject.

Such heated discussions made me try to talk myself out of doing this chapter. But if I'm to be true to the theme of what I wish I'd known before I was married, then this subject must be included. After all, I had no concept of biblical submission when Don and I publicly pledged our love to each other. I thought submission meant being a soft-spoken doormat. (I'm thankful that Don wasn't expecting that from me. He didn't seem frustrated at all that I wasn't the "doormat" type!) Over the years, Don and I walked together toward a greater understanding of what the Lord was calling us to. I learned that, rather than passively sitting by and letting her husband walk all over her, a wife is called to *actively choose* to allow her husband to take the responsibility as a servant/leader.

EVEN TODAY

Of course it's easy to say, "But this is the 1990s! Things are different now." Maybe. And I do agree that it's important that a couple be partners and make decisions together. But while agreement can usually be reached after much discussion and prayer, the time may come when the couple is still in disagreement and somebody will have to make the decision. That's when the wife should submit to the husband as the spiritual head of the house.

If you haven't tossed this book across the room yet, let me emphasize again that I'm not talking about being timid and a doormat, but choosing to give in to your husband's authority. Submission is an act of strength, not an act of weakness.

This view of the wife's role is supported, I believe, by the way Jesus treated women. He elevated women in a culture that treated them like property. He was kind to them, saw their hearts' needs, defended them from their male-centered society, and honored them by appearing to a woman after his resurrection. He obviously did not view women as second-rate.

I discussed this topic recently with my friend Jay Carty, president of Yes! Ministries. He explained the man's responsibility this way: When the couple can't agree, the husband must use his God-given responsibility as "tiebreaker." But he must make the decision based on what he is convinced is in his wife's best interest.

Tiebreaker, huh? I like that.

TRUE SUBMISSION

Let's take a minute and look at the Scripture that is causing so much discussion. Isn't it sad that one portion of Scripture gets more press than another? I wish more evangelical churches emphasized

Ephesians 5:21—"Submit to one another out of reverence for Christ"—but too often the featured text is Ephesians 5:22-33, which says,

> You wives will submit to your husbands as you do to the Lord. For a husband is the head of his wife as Christ is the head of his body, the church; he gave his life to be her Savior. As the church submits to Christ, so you wives must submit to your husbands in everything.
>
> And you husbands must love your wives with the same love Christ showed the church. He gave up his life for her to make her holy and clean, washed by baptism and God's word. He did this to present her to himself as a glorious church without a spot or wrinkle or any other blemish. Instead, she will be holy and without fault. In the same way, husbands ought to love their wives as they love their own bodies. For a man is actually loving himself when he loves his wife. No one hates his own body but lovingly cares for it, just as Christ cares for his body, which is the church. And we are his body.
>
> As the Scriptures say, "A man leaves his father and mother and is joined to his wife, and the two are united into one." This is a great mystery, but it is an illustration of the way Christ and the church are one. So again I say, each man must love his wife as he loves himself, and the wife must respect her husband.

I included the entire passage here because, as I told my friend in Dallas, I'm tired of two portions being overused without the context: *Wives submit and husbands love.*

As a youngster I attended churches where the pastors would preach for thirty minutes on the woman's duty to submit "no matter what." And their congregations—mostly women whose husbands were home sleeping off last night's drunk—absorbed his words and determined that "with God's help" they'd keep accepting the situation rather than getting help.

Those same pastors would then preach for a scant two minutes on the man's role—to love his wife as Christ loved the church. I remember one preacher who leaned forward at that point and said, "That means you're willing to die for her," and that was it. No explanation of Christ's sacrifice and selflessness and what it would really mean to follow his example.

The men seemed to relax, as though they were thinking, *Yeah, I fought in the war. I know how to protect my woman.*

I recently had an in-depth discussion about submission with my hairdresser, Michael Yates, as we waited for my color to take. (It's easy for women to talk to their hairdressers. After all, they see us at our worst!) Michael, a devoted husband and father, believes that men must be willing to lay down everything that's important as they take the role of servant/leader. "The principle of loving our wives as Christ loved the church is the toolbox that shows us how to love our wives as we should, but it doesn't come cheaply. It's a daily dying to self."

A *daily* dying to self. Setting aside his own desires, and sometimes even his needs, in order to love and care for his wife—as Christ did for the church. Seeking his wife's best interest and presenting that need to our heavenly Father. Wow. That makes the wife's role of submission easy.

WAIT FOR CONFIRMATION

Wise husbands know that submission works best when it's tempered with asking for the wife's confirmation of a decision. Gerald says the only way he'll move forward on any project is with Patsy's OK. And believe me, he's not "henpecked." He says he's learned the hard way that if he tries to go ahead without Patsy's confirmation, the Lord will not bless the project because it lacks unity.

Often, he says, Patsy may not be able to give reasons for her disapproval. She'll just *know*.

"I'd rather she tell me exactly why something won't work, but if she can't do that, then I'd still better listen," Gerald says. "When we were first married, I borrowed money to buy some business stock that was taking off. The company had recently secured a government contract, so I was convinced there was no place for this stuff to go but up.

"Well, then the president was indicted for fraud, and the stock fell so quickly that I couldn't sell in time to keep from losing most of the investment. Then I still had to pay back the money I'd borrowed to buy the stock in the first place. It took us a long time to regroup from that mistake, but to Patsy's credit, she never once said, 'I told you so.' I'm sure I wouldn't have reacted so graciously if she had made a mistake like that. You better believe I was ready to wait for her confirmation for every major decision after that.

"A few years later, I had an opportunity to buy a piece of property on the north side of town—just the direction the population was moving in—but Patsy didn't feel right about it. We'd prayed about it, the location was great, and I just knew this was what the Lord had for us. Patsy, though, refused to give me the needed confirmation. I was tempted to go ahead and buy it—kind of a 'Hey, I'm the man of the house' type of statement—but I kept remembering that can't-lose stock I'd lost on years before. I didn't buy the property, but I had my 'See, I told you so' speech all set for later."

He shook his head. "The property sold quickly and then was immediately offered for resale at a profit of $26,000. I was getting a little hot under the collar, thinking of what I could have had, but the prospective buyer asked for an environmental check before he'd close on the deal. The ground testing showed that the area had been used as an unauthorized chemical dump years ago. That made the property useless!

"The prospective buyer quickly backed out," he added. "That

left the original buyer with only two choices: abandon the land and lose the purchase price or do an environmental cleanup that cost so much that it would take years to recoup his original purchase price. Ouch! I really feel sorry for the guy because I know that could have just as easily been me—if I hadn't been spiritually mature enough to wait for Patsy's confirmation."

But what if Gerald had gone ahead and purchased the property without Patsy's approval? I'm convinced that as long as it wasn't immoral or illegal, she would have had to submit to her husband's authority, praying all the while that if she was wrong the Lord would show her and that if she was right the Lord would keep them from disaster. Sometimes the Lord allows a wrong move to be made—for his purpose.

AN EARLY LESSON

In 1927, my own beloved grandparents, Papa and Mama Farley, had to face that same type of challenge. Papa—my gentle little Irish grandfather—decided he was going to buy a farm in Indiana even though my grandmother didn't feel right about it. They prayed about the move, Mama shared her misgivings, but still Papa said they were going.

Mama was a woman of enormous emotional strength, so some of the well-meaning relatives suggested that she put her foot down and insist they stay in Kentucky.

But Mama shook her head and said, "It's something he has to do. If we don't go, he'll always wonder. At least this way, he'll know."

And with that, she cheerfully packed household goods and eight children and set off like a pioneer woman for greener pastures and better farmland.

None of the relatives found out the details, but when Mama asked Papa to uncrate the piano, he looked past her to the field beyond their porch and quietly said, "There's no need. We won't be staying."

A few months later, they were back in Kentucky, and Papa was saying he'd never "go off" again. He was still very much the head of that household for the rest of their lives together, but he more openly trusted Mama's insight and waited for her confirmation before going ahead with any major decision.

I used that incident as an encouragement recently when one of my young friends was determined that she wasn't going to move to another state with her husband, who wanted to buy a business tied in with tourism. We women are security oriented, and we need to have our nest around us just so. I understand that all too well, but my friend's digging in her heels and refusing to move was causing such tension with her husband that she was going to lose either way: If she moved, she was going to have to give up the house that she dearly loved and had fixed up so nicely. But if she didn't move, she was going to lose her husband.

She had heard many of my Mama Farley stories on our noon walks, so I pulled out the moving-to-Indiana story and ended by saying, "It's like Mama said, 'It's something he has to do.' If you don't go, he's always going to resent you for keeping him from his dream. This way he'll know. And if the plan fails, it won't be *your* fault. You're going to lose something either way. I vote that you lose a beloved house rather than a beloved husband. I don't recommend being a single parent at all!"

So they moved and have had wild adjustments to make in their new surroundings, but he's having a wonderful time—and is the happiest she's seen him in years. She agrees that that counts for something. And she's adjusting as well—and discovering that there is life outside of Colorado.

A Husband's Godly Example

Another important ingredient in the submission-love mix is a husband who leads by godly example.

One Saturday morning, Don received a church call saying a family needed a mattress. They had the bed frames and springs, but could we help with a mattress?

We certainly could. In fact, we had just taken down our antique guest bed to put up a crib for our newborn daughter, Holly. The pristine white mattress with the big blue flowers had been slept on only twice and was now stored under blankets in our basement. Of course we'd donate it.

Don called the family to let them know he and a buddy would be out that afternoon to deliver the mattress. When would be a good time? They settled on three o'clock.

But when Don and John arrived at exactly three o'clock, no one answered their knock. Just as they stepped off the porch to return to the station wagon, a neighbor ran over.

"Oh, they're gone, but they asked me to watch for you. I've got a key; you can just bring the mattress in this side door."

So Don and John pulled the mattress out of the vehicle and lugged it into the house.

The smell of cat urine and burned food hit them as soon as they opened the door. The neighbor gestured toward a filthy wall nearby and said, "They said just to leave it here. They'll take care of it later."

Don looked at the filth as conflicting thoughts bumped through his mind: *How ungrateful these people are that they didn't even stay around after we'd agreed on the time. And now they want me to lean my spotless mattress against that filthy wall.*

Then in his heart, he said, *Lord, I can't give these people this mattress.*

He said later that it was almost as though the Lord answered in that moment, "Then give it to *me*" and wrapped Don in an incredible peace that made even the intense smells fade.

Don replied, *OK, Lord. This mattress is yours. If you want your mattress left in a filthy place, then I guess that's your business.* And he and John leaned the mattress against the wall and left.

When Don told me the account, he didn't know it would stay with me for all of these years. In fact, that story guided me through the letting go of many things after his death, especially when the kiddos and I moved to New York so I could start a new career—and a new adventure with the Lord. Don set the example, and he lived out his faith in the midst of struggle. And that counts with me. I'm not much to listen when folks who have never struggled tell me, "Just give it to Jesus," when they've never had to give anything to him—and I'm not just talking about mattresses, either. Untried virtue is no virtue!

Don also displayed incredible strength when he was going through his cancer treatments. If I'm ever faced with that type of challenge in my own health, his example will stand with me.

When the cancer came out of remission, the doctors decided to do a lumbar puncture. They would draw out spinal fluid and replace it with the same amount of chemotherapy.

That night the doctor turned away from Don and looked at me. "Mrs. Aldrich, please wait outside," he said.

I looked directly at him. "No. I'm going to sit in this corner. And when you see my head down, ignore me. I won't be passed out; I'll be praying."

He moved toward the bed without another word.

For thirty minutes I prayed silently as they made repeated attempts to find that spot between the vertebrae where the needle had to go. But Don's side pain from the shingles that had developed during the course of his cancer wasn't allowing him to pull his body into the proper curl position. With each of his low moans, my stomach tightened that much more. Finally I stood up and faced the doctors.

"OK, I've had it. Now you *better* let me help. I'm through listening to you hurt him."

The resident glanced at the intern. "All right," he said. "Maybe if you pulled him into a tight curl. His spine has just enough curvature to make it difficult to insert the needle properly."

I leaned down and kissed Don's perspiration-soaked cheek.

"Come on, Donnie. We'll do it this time."

My right arm went around his shoulders, my left one under his knees. Bracing my legs against the bed, I pulled with all my Kentucky might.

"That's it!" the doctor said. "Now hold him just like that." For an eternity neither of us moved. Every fiber in my shoulders screamed for release. *If only I could move just a little. . . . No, just a few more minutes.*

With my mouth close to Don's ear I whispered prayers. "Thank you, Lord, for being with us. Thank you for the goodness you will bring out of this."

Somehow the minutes passed, and he was allowed to uncurl. Both doctors nodded their thanks to me. Apparently they passed the word along, too—in future lumbar punctures, even the new interns waited for me to take my position before beginning the procedure.

I always prayed in his ear to take our minds off of our separate pains, but at one point, my shoulder muscles were burning so badly that I had to stop to take a breath. As I did I realized that my beloved Scotsman was singing ever so softly, "What a friend we have in Jesus, all our sins and griefs to bear. What a privilege to carry everything to God in prayer."

I tried to keep my tears from falling on his face, but I knew he had just given me another example of his godly strength. So there! That's the type of man to whom it is easy to submit.

MAKE A CHOICE

As Jay, Holly, and I moved from New York to Colorado, we stopped at the Illinois homestead of Abraham Lincoln's parents.

The workers there portrayed people who would have been on the nineteenth-century farm. It was a hot August day, and the women, in their heavy skirts, were taking food from the open fireplace. The men were already seated at a large table set up on sawhorses under a shady tree.

As I looked out at the men seated while the women lifted the cast-iron pots off the iron hooks in that hot kitchen, I teased the woman nearest me, "The men are just sitting out there while you do all the work," I said. "I don't know if I'd serve them."

Still in character, she retorted, "Well, it's plain to see *you* don't have a man!"

My jaw dropped. She was right! I quickly became interested in a piece of pottery on the nearby shelf.

I thought of her recently when I heard that Candy and Edwin were in the process of a divorce. When I first met them, Candy struck me as a wanna-be "liberated woman," since she told me, "Call me Candy or *Ms.,* but not *Mrs."*

As I got to know them better, I learned that Candy refused to cook for Edwin, demanded that he do his own laundry, and refused to respect him as the head of their home. I was appalled. I may be feisty, but I have the good sense to know that is not the way marriage works best. It's two people working together to help each other be all that God wants them to be.

Need I tell you that Edwin finally decided that wasn't the way marriage should be either? He and Candy are now divorced. How sad. And it didn't have to be like that.

EVERY CIRCUS ...
Remember Brian, at the beginning of this chapter, and his comment that every circus needs a ringmaster?

I was so intrigued by his ringmaster comparison that I called a major circus, headquartered in Florida, to get some information about the actual duties of a ringmaster. I connected with a delightful buyer named Dave, who enjoyed educating me about circus life. When I asked about the ringmaster's duties, he chuckled.

"Oh, he's the 'pretty boy'—he's out there to announce and sing and look good," he said. "But in a large circus like ours, it's actually the performance director who is timing the acts and keeping things moving right along."

That was news to me, and I told him so. Dave continued, "Oh, sure. He's the guy dressed in a tux on the sidelines, carrying a clipboard and a watch. Both the ringmaster and the performance director are equipped with whistles, so if something goes wrong with an act, either one can blow that thing and get the clowns out to take the audience's attention away from the problem. Both of them have equal power, but only the ringmaster is in the spotlight."

I had fun pondering an analogy to the marriage relationship: The husband may be "in the limelight" as far as being the visible head of the home, but any well-run circus, even marriage, needs both a ringmaster and a performance director. As Dave said, they both have equal power, and either one can blow the whistle that calls in help when there's a problem.

Hmmm. Ringmaster in the limelight, getting the credit. Performance director keeping things on track. And both equipped for an emergency. The implications for marriage are almost delicious.

A FINAL WORD

A few summers ago, while working at a clothing store, Holly overheard a wife ask her husband if she could buy a particular article of clothing. When Holly got home, she asked, "Will I have to ask my husband's permission to buy clothing?"

I looked at her for a long moment, then said, "Yes, if you value your relationship with him."

She sighed. "OK, but what if I'm making a good salary, too?"

"Holly, don't think of it as 'asking permission' but as showing respect for your husband—for what he likes, for how he feels—just asking for his input because he's important to you," I said. "Think 'relationship,' not 'permission.' That will get you through the rough spots."

Let's stop arguing over the literal meaning of submission and concentrate on making our marriage the best that it can be, based on love for the Lord, love for each other, and mutual respect. This is a tough world; let's go forward together, determined to make it a better place, starting within our own home.

SIMPLE REMINDERS

1. "Equal partnership sounds good in theory, but in practice somebody has to run the show."
2. When the situation has been prayed through and still no agreement is forthcoming, the husband has the responsibility of being the tiebreaker.
3. As tiebreaker, the husband is to make the decision based on what he believes will be in his wife's best interest.
4. What if we put more emphasis on Ephesians 5:21— "Submit to one another out of reverence for Christ"?
5. Wise husbands wait for confirmation from the Lord through their wives.
6. Men, want us to submit? Then be the godly leaders you have been called to be. Even a feisty Christian woman wants her husband to take the spiritual leadership that is his privilege.
7. Wives, think "relationship" not "permission."
8. Let's stop arguing over the literal meaning of "submit" and concentrate on making our marriage the best it can be.

DISCUSSION QUESTIONS

1. What background in submission did you bring to your marriage?
2. What was your greatest challenge in this area?
3. How do you decide what the Lord's will is for your family in any given area?
4. How are you teaching your children about submission both to authority and to one another?
5. What advice do you have for couples struggling in this area?

NOTES

Chapter 2. Hey! This Is Hard Work!

1. Patricia McGerr, "Johnny Lingo's Eight-Cow Wife," *Reader's Digest* (February 1988): 138.
2. Jerry Jenkins, *Hedges: Loving Your Marriage Enough to Protect It* (Brentwood, Tenn.: Wolgemuth and Hyatt, Publishers, Inc., 1989), 28.

Chapter 5. Men Read Newspapers, Not Minds

1. This material is now available in print: Gary D. Chapman, Ph.D., *The Five Love Languages* (Chicago: Northfield Publishing, 1992). Used by permission.
2. James C. Dobson, *Love for a Lifetime* (Sisters, Oreg.: Multnomah Books, 1987, 1993), 57.
3. Willard F. Harley Jr., *His Needs, Her Needs* (Grand Rapids, Mich.: Revell, 1994), 12–13.

Chapter 6. Adults Are Just Tall Children

1. Interview with author, first reported in "David Meece: Singing through the Pain," *Christian Herald* (April 1989): 14.

Chapter 7. Battle the Battle, Not Each Other

1. Carole Mayhall, "Words to Avoid in Marriage," *Today's Christian Woman* (July/August 1994): 42.

Chapter 8. Whaddaya Mean, I'm Overdrawn—*Again?*

1. Jane Bryant Quinn, "Money Facts," *Woman's Day* (Sept. 24, 1991): 14.
2. Stephen Advokat, "Sacrifice, Strategy Key When Reducing Income," *Colorado Springs Gazette Telegraph,* 1 May 1995, C6.
3. Lindsey O'Connor, *Working at Home* (Eugene, Oreg.: Harvest House, 1990).

Chapter 9. How Do I Stop This Runaway Train?

1. LynNell Hancock, et al., "Breaking Point," *Newsweek* (6 March 1995): 56.

Chapter 10. Serving the Lord by Serving Others

1. Billie Wilson, "When Prayer Wasn't Enough," *Christian Herald* (July/August 1988): 24.
2. Christine Scheele, "Mile High Hope," *Christian Herald* (May 1989): 10.
3. Dean Merrill and Larry Byars, "No Small Potatoes," *Christian Herald* (March 1988): 37.
4. Sandra P. Aldrich, *From One Single Mother to Another* (Ventura, Calif: Gospel Light/Regal Books, 1991), 179.